The House Church
In the Writings of Paul

The House Church
In the Writings of Paul

by

Vincent P. Branick

WIPF & STOCK · Eugene, Oregon

About the Author

Vincent Branick, received a S.S.D. from the Pontifical Biblical Institute in Rome and a S.T.L. and Ph.D. in Philosophy from the University of Fribourg, Switzerland. He is presently Professor of Religious Studies at the University of Dayton. He is author of *Wonder in a Technical World,* editor of *Mary, The Spirit, and The Church,* and the author of several scholarly articles in the *Catholic Biblical Quarterly* and the *Journal of Biblical Literature.*

Wipf and Stock Publishers
199 W 8th Ave, Suite 3
Eugene, OR 97401

The House Church in the Writings of Paul
By Branick, Vincent
Copyright©1989 by Branick, Vincent
ISBN 13: 978-1-62032-029-7
Publication date 3/1/2012
Previously published by Michael Glazier, 1989

Dedicated with love
to
Marie

Table of Contents

Editor's Note

Zacchaeus Studies provide concise, readable and relatively inexpensive scholarly studies on particular aspects of scripture and theology. The New Testament section of the series presents studies dealing with focal or debated questions; and the volumes focus on specific texts of particular themes of current interest in biblical interpretation. Specialists have their professional journals and other forums where they discuss matters of mutual concern, exchange ideas and further contemporary trends of research; and some of their work on contemporary biblical research is now made accessible for students and others in *Zacchaeus Studies*.

The authors in this series share their own scholarship in non-technical language, in the areas of their expertise and interest. These writers stand with the best in current biblical scholarship in the English-speaking world. Since most of them are teachers, they are accustomed to presenting difficult material in comprehensible form without compromising a high level of critical judgment and analysis.

The works of this series are ecumenical in content and purpose and cross credal boundaries. They are designed to augment formal and informal biblical study and discussion. Hopefully they will also serve as texts to enhance and supplement seminary, university and college classes. The series will also aid Bible study groups, adult education and parish religious education classes to develop intelligent, versatile and challenging programs for those they serve.

Mary Ann Getty RSM
New Testament Editor

Introduction

The discovery in 1932 of "the Christian building" in the ancient Roman garrison town of Dura-Europos, now on the eastern borders of Syria, stimulated interest in the house church of the New Testament. Here was basically a private house which was used as a church. Dated from the 3rd century, the ruins remain the earliest and most complete Christian church excavated.

In 1938 and 1939 two articles appeared in the *Journal of Biblical Literature* dealing in their own ways with New Testament house churches. Donald W. Riddle published, "Early Christian Hospitality. A Factor in the Gospel Transmission."[1] The following year Floyd V. Filson wrote, "The Significance of the Early House Churches."[2] Filson pointed out the need for much more study on the Christian house church, a sentiment still repeated in more recent studies on this topic.

An impetus was given to interest in the topic by recent sociological approaches to the New Testament. The works of Gerd Theissen, many of which are conveniently collected in *The Social Setting of Pauline Christianity*,[3] and more recently those of Wayne Meeks, especially *The First Urban Christians*.

---

[1] *Journal of Biblical Literature* [*JBL*], 57 (1938), 141-154.
[2] *JBL*, 58 (1939), 105-112.
[3] trans. J. Schuetz; Philadelphia: Fortress, 1982.

The Social World of the Apostle Paul,[4] are among the most important in the application of sociological questions and problematics to early Christian writings. As questions were raised dealing with the internal authority structure of the family, the social stratification of families according to wealth and property and the voluntary associations which formed an intermediary between household and city, the picture of the house church began to appear with clearer details and colors.

Two book length studies on the house church appeared almost simultaneously in 1981: Robert Banks, *Paul's Idea of Community: The Early House Churches in their Historical Setting*[5] and Hans-Josef Klauck, *Hausgemeinde und Hauskirche im fruehen Christentum.*[6] The present study is heavily indebted to these books.

In 1964 the Second Vatican Council appeared to make an oblique allusion to the house church by referring to the family as "so to speak the domestic church" (*Lumen Gentium,* 11). The Council was thinking of the role of parents as the first preachers of the faith by word and example to their children. Nothing was said about official ecclesial functioning on the level of the family nor about any way the family fitted into the complex interrelationship between local (i.e. diocesan) church and world-wide church. Nevertheless after the Council "home Masses" quickly multiplied, at least in the United States. In South America *communidades de base,* groups of families who gather together for church and social support, developed showing distinct resemblances to the New Testament house church.

The study of the house church, we will see, takes us to the heart of many basic issues in early Christianity. We will focus on Paul's churches, but we must look to other later texts, both New Testament and extra-biblical, for insights and hints about

[4]New Haven: Yale, 1983.

[5]Grand Rapids: Eerdmans, 1980.

[6]Stuttgarter Bibelstudien, 103 Stuttgart: Verlag Katholisches Biblework, 1981.

the nature of these communities. Because the existence of such house churches was not an issue for him, Paul says little directly about them as such. His instructions about church life, however, become more understandable when read from the perspective of a household community and at the same time shed light on these groups.

Our study will begin with a look at Paul's references to the private house churches in an effort to situate this small community in Paul's larger view of both the local church, which also met in some respects as a house church, and his view of a world-wide church (chapter 1). After this overview of Paul, we will attempt to catch a glimpse at the historical context of the house churches, studying the nature of houses and households of the Greco-Roman world along with other parallels to the local churches (chapter 2). Returning to the New Testament texts, our next steps will identify both the prominent people in Paul's world who could have hosted house churches (chapter 3) as well as the incipient offices that gave structure to the private house church and the local church (chapter 4). We will then pull together the details that describe the activities that took place during the church gatherings (chapter 5). Finally, we will attempt to reconstruct the forces and events that led to the disappearance of the house church (chapter 6).

The published sources for most of the classical authors cited, both Latin and Greek, is the Loeb Classical Library. The English translations of the New Testament are all mine. To bring out the particular aspect under study, I often needed to produce a special, even wooden, translation of the original. What I sacrifice in literary grace I hope I gain in accuracy. Most of the other block quotes from Latin, Greek, or Syriac texts are also my translations.

Vincent P. Branick, SS.D.
Dayton, Ohio

1

The Christian Household in Paul's Theology of Church

"Aquila and Prisca with their house church (*syn tē kat' oikon autōn ekklēsia*) send abundant greetings in the Lord," Paul writes to the Corinthians from Ephesus (1 Cor 16:19). Some three years later writing to Rome, Paul again states, "Give my greetings to Prisca and Aquila ... and to their house church" (*tēn kat' oikon autōn ekklēsian,* Rom 16:3.5). Writing from prison toward the end of his career, Paul sends a note to his friend Philemon. Opening the letter in his conventional way, Paul greets Philemon, his wife Apphia, Archippus, possibly thier son, and "your house church" (*tē kat' oikon sou ekklēsia,* Phlm 2). Finally in the letter to the Colossians, which Paul probably commissioned before his death, we find greetings to Nympha in neighboring Laodicea and "to her house church" (*tēn kat' oikon autēs ekklēsian,* Col 4:15). The four greetings are the four instances in which Paul speaks explicitly of house churches, assemblies of Christians that formed in and around a private household.

These greetings remind us that the earliest Christians met in private homes. For them the household with its family setting was the church. Out of that household arose some of the earliest offices and structures that would shape the course of the church through the centuries.

The private dwelling functioned for the church on two levels. It formed the environment for house churches strictly speaking,

13

gatherings of Christians around one family in the home of that family. The four greetings above are directed to or come from such house churches. On a second broader level, the private dwelling formed the environment for gatherings of the local church, the assembly of all the Christian households and individuals of a city. For such a group the home functioned as a house church, since the building remained the domicile of the host family.

Most probably Paul did not found any of the single family house churches that he greets. He apparently did not establish any churches in the area of Colossae and Laodicea, including the house churches of Philemon and Nympha. Prisca and Aquila founded their house church in Rome long before Paul arrived. This Christian couple likewise was sufficiently independent of Paul, as we shall see, that they probably established their house church in Ephesus on their own.

Other early Christian groups outside the Pauline circle met in private houses. First Peter, most probably written from Rome, likewise includes much indirect evidence of house churches.[1] Luke describes house meetings as precisely the activity distinguishing the earliest Jerusalem believers from Jewish non-Christians. With their Jewish compatriots, these members of "the Way" worshiped in the Temple, "while breaking bread at home" (*kat'oikon,* Acts 2:46; cf. 5:42). The Christian home appears here in exact counterpoint to the Jewish Temple.

As with most "foreign" cults in their earliest stages of expansion, the Christian meeting in private homes was probably a practical necessity. For the Christians the synagogues quickly became off limits. The pagan temples involved too many unsavory associations. And the stately basilicas were centuries away. The private home on the other hand afforded a place of privacy, intimacy, and stability for the early Christians.

For about a century the private dwelling shaped the Christians' community life, forming the environment in which Chris-

---

[1]cf. John Elliot, *A Home for the Homeless. A Sociological Exegesis of 1 Peter, its Situation and Strategy* (Philadelphia: Fortress, 1981).

tians related to each other, providing an economic substructure for the community, a platform for missionary work, a framework for leadership and authority, and probably a definite role for women. Above all the private home and specifically the dining room (*triclinium* or *diwan*) provided an environment that corresponded remarkably with the Christians' earliest self-identification, reflecting Jesus' own choice of an "upper room" for his last supper, his own choice of "non-sacred space" as the environment of his work, and his insistence on familial ties among believers.

Sometime in the second half of the second century, Christians began to dedicate their homes to church assembly. The building ceased to be a residence. Modifications to the structure turned the dining room into a larger assembly hall. Other rooms assumed community functions. Although resembling a house, the building became a church. Eventually Christians were allowed to rebuild their churches from the ground. In AD 314, a year after the Edict of Milan, the first of the basilicas appeared.

The Christians meeting in the dedicated churches and basilicas show an understanding of themselves different from that of the Christians meeting in the house churches. Leadership became concentrated in fewer hands, the hands of a special class of holy people. Church activities became stylized ritual. The building rather than the community became the temple of God. Whether environment determines ideology or ideology determines environment, the link between the two is clear when we examine the shift from the house church to the dedicated church.

Our study will look at the times when Christians met exclusively in private households. More specifically we will focus on the times and churches of Paul. We will look at the connections which appear between the household setting for the churches and the self-understanding and activities of these churches. Of particular interest will be the relationship between the private house church and the local church, a relationship which seemed to create powerful tensions for Christian leaders like Paul. Following the lead of Paul, our study will refer to

the smaller unit as "house church" or church *kat' oikon.* We will speak of the larger units—which also met in private houses—as the local or city-wide church.

1. Family and Household Terminology in Paul

The frequency of family and household terminology in Paul for the Christian community is striking. He addresses or refers to his fellow Christians as "brother," *adelphos,* 114 times, expressing the basic relationship that should hold sway among believers (cf. esp. 1 Cor 8:11.13; 15:58; Rom 15:14; Phil 2:25; 3:1; 4:1; Col 4:7; Phlm 7). He uses "sister," *adelphē,* 5 times. The term "brother" may have some technical nuance in the ten or so references by Paul to his co-workers (Gal 1:2; 1 Cor 1:1; 16:20; 2 Cor 1:1; 2:13; 8:23; 9:3.5; Phil 2:25; Col 1:2; 4:15).

At other times Paul identifies himself as a parent to the communities. He exhorts the Thessalonians "as a father to his children" (1 Thess 2:11), an image he repeats when writing to the Corinthians (1 Cor 4:14-15). Onesimus he describes as "my child whom he begot in chains" (Phlm 10). Timothy is to Paul "as a son with his father" (Phil 2:22). He sees himself also as pregnant mother bearing the Galatians (Gal 4:19; cf. I Thess 2:7), imagery which does not prevent him from relating to the mother of Rufus as "his mother and mine" (Rom 16:13).

When Paul speaks of "building up" the community (1 Thess 5:11; 1 Cor 8:1.10; 10:23; 14:3-5.12.17.26; 2 Cor 10:8; 12:19; 13:10; Rom 14:19; 15:2), he generally uses the Greek word *oikodomē,* derived from the Greek word for "house," *oikos.* Similarly he addresses the Galatians as "the household," *oi oikeioi,* of the faith (Gal 6:10). He himself is the "steward," *oikonomos* of the mysteries of God (1 Cor 4:1-2), entrusted with the administration, *oikonomia,* of the gospel, terms drawn from the business side of family affairs. Even his description of himself as the "wise architect," *sophos architektōn,* laying the foundation of the community (1 Cor 3:10-13) belongs to this linguistic context of house building.

This household and familial terminology has its roots in the Old Testament and the Judaism in which Paul grew up. Israel

was a "house" or "household" (*oikos Israel, bet Yisrael,* cf. Amos 5:25; Jer 38:33), although Israel was never called "the household of God." Israelites were "brothers" (Lev 10:4; 19:17; Deut 15:3). The teacher of wisdom often spoke to the disciple as "son" (Sir 2:1; 3:12.17; 4:1; 6:18.24.32). Wisdom herself spoke to her children (Sir 4:11). Similarly the Essene overseer was as a "father" to his "children."[2] The Qumran community identified itself as the "household of truth," "of holiness," "of perfection," and its members as "sons of the light," "of truth," "of righteousness," "of heaven."[3]

Household and family terminology used for a religious group thus precedes Paul and his application of this terminology to the house church experience. The frequency and pervasiveness of this language in Paul, however, indicates that for him the words were not empty religious formulas. Household language far exceeds words borrowed from cult, religion, or any other institution to describe the interpersonal relationships. Paul is not prophet, priest, or commander. He is an apostle and a father to his communities who are families. The practical necessity of meeting in private homes clearly blended with Paul's theological understanding of the Christian community.

Paul lived this family relationship with his co-workers and communities and he wanted them to live the same. His admonitions could ring strong in the communities because the nucleus of the community was in fact the family. The church began with the intimate and intense interpersonal relationships of family members. As Robert Banks states, "Given the family character of the Christian community, the homes of its members provided the most conducive atmosphere in which they could give expression to the bond they had in common."[4]

[2] CD 13:9.

[3] 1QS 1:9; 3:13.20.22.25; 4:5-6:22; 8:5.9; CD 3:19.

[4] Banks, *Paul's Idea of Community,* p. 61.

2. The Household in Mission Strategy

Most probably the conversion of a household and the consequent formation of a house church formed the key element in Paul's strategic plan to spread the Gospel to the world. If we follow Acts in this matter, Paul had little success preaching in the synagogues. His method then shifted to establishing himself with a prominent family, which then formed his base of operations in a given city (cf. Acts 16:13-34; 17:2-9; 18:1-11).

It is not surprising then to see frequent mention of baptisms, not just of individuals, but of whole households. Paul mentions such a conversion once (1 Cor 1:16). The Acts makes such a household conversion almost a theme in itself (Acts 10:2; 16:15; 16:33; 18:8; cf. also Jn 4:53).

We can probably suppose some social pressure on individuals within a household to convert with the conversion of the head of that house. To the degree such pressure existed, the conversion of a household to Christianity would entail a diversity of personal conviction and engagement.

In any case, hospitality was the key to the mission. Paul's work was characterized by mobility and travel. In order to accomplish his mission, he depended on an extensive network of social relationships, centered on households. Hospitality to Paul meant not only material support but also attachment to his gospel. It meant sharing his work. Such ideological support appears especially in Paul's reflection on the Philippians' financial subvention of his work (Phil 4:14-18; 2 Cor 8:1-5).

Paul frequently refers to "receiving" (*prosdechesthai*) his co-workers and "sending" (*propempein*) them on their way (Rom 16:1-2; Phil 2:27-29). These words are part of an almost technical language describing the local group's part in the mission. The local group was to accord hospitality to Paul's emissary and then provide that person with enough assistance to return to Paul or to reach the next station.

Centuries later in his *Commentary on Philemon*, St. Jerome described hospitality to Paul as participating in Paul's apostleship:

[Philemon] was to prepare a guest place more for the apostle than for Paul. When Paul would arrive at a new city to preach the crucified one and to proclaim a teaching never heard before, he had to meet many persons. For this he needed before anything an appropriate place in the city where all could gather, a place without disturbances, large in order to receive many listeners, not near the places of spectacles nor with disturbing neighbors.[5]

Jerome seems to have in mind more the basilicas and *aulae* of his day when describing the "large" rooms where "all could gather," instead of the private guest room which Paul actually requests from Philemon. Nevertheless, Jerome reflects a church memory which accurately connected early Christian hospitality with missionary work.

The same connection can be found in the gospel accounts of Jesus' instructions to apostles as he sent them out to preach, "Into whatever house (*oikia*) you enter, remain there until you leave" (Mk 6:10). Luke's rendition of the instruction is more explicit, "Into whatever city you go, after they welcome you, eat what they set before you and cure the sick there" (Lk 10:8-9). Such an instruction implies a full incorporation into the household. A household formed the base of operations. The key to the mission was acceptance by one household.

In effect, then, the missionary effort described in the gospels involves two manners of following Jesus. One manner is explicit:

> Take nothing for the journey, neither walking staff nor traveling bag; no bread, no money. No one is to have two coats. Into whatever household you enter, stay there and proceed from there (Lk 9:3).

> Stop worrying, "What are we to eat? What are we to drink? What are we to wear?.... Seek first the kingdom and God's justice, and all these things will be given to you (Matt 6:31-33).

---

[5]ad v.22; PL 26/616b.

Such is the life style of the itinerant and propertyless missionary, following Jesus, who has nowhere of his own to lay his head (Matt 8:20; Lk 9:58). The second manner of following Jesus is not as clearly portrayed in the gospels, but is clearly demanded as the presupposition of the first life-style. This is the manner of the host into whose household the itinerant missionary is received. This is the life-style of the providers of the "hundred-fold households, and brothers, and sisters, and mothers, and children and fields" which the propertyless followers receive "now in this present age" (Mk 10:30). The home was thus something a follower of Jesus either leaves behind or opens for the use of the Gospel.

The house or home figured prominently in the mission of Jesus himself as described in the Synoptics. Jesus often gives special teaching *en oikō*, at home (Mk 2:1; 7:14-27; 9:33; 10:2-12; Matt 13:36). Jesus himself acts as a host (Mk 2:15; 6:34-44; 8:1-10; Lk 12:37). Luke frequently portrays him as a guest in a home (Lk 5:29; 7:36-50; 9:53; 10:38; 14:1; cf. also Mk 1:29; 3:20; 9:33).

These Synoptic portrayals, closely linking the missions of both Jesus and the disciples with homes, may in fact reflect historical memories about Jesus and the first disciples. The stress that this link between mission and home receives in the gospels, however, indicates a similar link in the communities producing these gospels. From the number of times especially in the Gospel of Mark that we see Jesus giving special instructions at home, we can conclude that the catechetical practices of the Marcan church in particular developed in and around home life.

3. Leadership

The house church thus functioned as the nucleus of the Christian community. Philosophers had long regarded the household as the basic unit of society.[6] Larger than our modern

---

[6]cf. Aristotle, *Politics*, 1952 b 9-19; Plutarch, *Life of Lycurgus*, 19,2.

"nuclear family," the household was a basis of economic activity, involving clients and business partners. It was a reflection of the political authority of the state or *polis*. The head of the household stood in the place of the king and represented that household to the wider political unit.

The adaptation of the church to the household entailed important consequences, particularly for the leadership of the community, a topic that will occupy our attention in greater detail later in this study. We can generally presume that the head of the household would exercise important authority over the Christian group of that household. At the last supper, Jesus functioned more or less as the father in a family. A household head or *paterfamilias* would have legal responsibility for the group meeting in his house. Luke gives us an example of that responsibility in the story of Paul at the house of Jason in Thessalonica. Jason gets into serious trouble for hosting Paul and Silas and must post bail for the socially unacceptable behavior of his house guests (Acts 17:6-9). Later when the church office of presbyter-bishop developed, candidates were judged by their ability to function as a *paterfamilias* (1 Tim 3:4-5; Tit 1:6).

The natural dominance of the *paterfamilias* in a house church would explain much of the later patriarchalism in the church. To the degree the church was assumed into the household, it was incorporated into a structure of authority, in which the father functioned in the place of the ruler. Even when the church is loosened from the household, its leaders will maintain the aura of "Father."

On the other hand, within the house church the mother of the family most likely functioned in a significant way. The mother in many ways was the manager of the household. The widow often stood in the place of her deceased spouse for business activities. Most probably, the mother would not have been reduced to a passive spectator in the church that met in her house.

In fact we notice a conspicuous mention of women in connection with the house church. Nympha appears as the patron of her church (Col 4:15). Apphia is mentioned in connection with Paul's greeting to Philemon and his house church (Phlm

1-2). Paul is careful to mention Prisca even before naming her husband Aquila in connection with their house church (Rom 16:3.5; 1 Cor 16:9; cf. Acts 18:2.18; 2 Tim 4:19).

4. The House Church in the Larger Community

The house church, on the one hand, and the household gathered in prayer, on the other, did not simply coincide. This is clear from Paul's own writings. Not every member of a family became Christian when the head of the house did. Until he fled his master and met Paul, Onesimus, the slave of Christian Philemon, was not a Christian (Phlm 10). Paul lays down precise norms for families where the spouses are not both believers (1 Cor 7:12-16). Likewise, Paul addresses Christian groups in households apparently headed by non-Christians. For instance the greeting to the "members of the household of Narcissus who are in the Lord" (Rom 16:11) appears to be a greeting to a specific Christian group within an otherwise non-Christian household. People who converted individually probably attached themselves to existing Christian households.

This lack of perfect coincidence between the house church and the household lay at the basis of the openness of the churches to each other, the networking of house churches into some form of city-wide federation we can call "the local church." The relationship between "the single family church" and "the local church" was not clear-cut and finely drawn. Paul makes no attempt to relate "house church" to "local church." From the start a house church of a particular family could well have involved others from non-Christian households. Likewise for some time a single house church of a particular family may have been the only church of a locality. Only gradually, as house churches multiplied in a locality, would the reality of "local church" take on distinct definition. Yet because the meeting of a local church would take place in a house church, the larger unit would still reflect the smaller.

On the whole Paul seems to emphasize the formation of the local church, allowing the house church of the individual family

to recede into the background. Given the strategy of the early missionaries and the constraints against meeting in other places, the appearance of the "single family" house church was to a degree a natural development. The networking of these house churches into a local church appears to be the object of a special effort on the part of Paul.

Paul's most frequent use of the term "church" refers to a local, i.e. city-wide group of Christians. This meaning is clearest where Paul attaches the name of a city to the word. Paul twice greets "the church of God which is in Corinth" (1 Cor 1:2; 2 Cor 1:1). Similarly he greets "the church of the Thessalonians" (1 Thess 1:1; cf. 2 Thess 1:1). In Romans, Paul describes Phoebe's role in "the church of Cenchreae," a port village just outside of Corinth (Rom 16:1). Colossians also refers to the "church of the Laodiceans" (4:16). Although he does not address the Philippians as "the church which is in Philippi," Paul describes them obliquely as a church when he states, "No church became a partner with me in matters of giving and receiving except you alone" (Phil 4:15).

Paul refers to the city-wide church with the expression, *holē tē ekklēsia*, "the whole church," the counterpart of an *ekklêsia kat' oikon*, a house church. The English cognate "catholic" employs the Greek expression *kath' holē*, but the church *kath' holē* for Paul was the city-wide or local assembly, not some world-wide organization. Thus Paul speaks of the situation in Corinth of an outsider entering the assembly "when the whole church (*hē ekklēsia holē*) is gathered in the same place" (1 Cor 14:23). Again writing from Corinth to the Romans Paul sends greetings from Gaius and distinguishes him as "host to me and to the whole church" (*holēs tēs ekklēsias*, Rom 16:23).

Another expression of Paul which indicates a plenary meeting of the local church is the description of the Christians "gathering at the same place" (*synerchomenōn epi to auto*). Paul describes such an assembly for "the Lord's Supper" in Corinth (1 Cor 11:20).

In his two references to "the whole church," the stress on the plenary character of the gathering suggests something special about the event. "The whole church in the same place" sounds like an important event. Likewise, redundancy of the expression, "to gather in the same place," seems to point to a special assembly. Gaius is singled out for special mention due to his generosity in gathering the whole Corinthian church at his house. It would appear that the Corinthians did not always meet at his house.

If the plenary assemblies of the Corinthian church were special, we can infer the existence of sub-groups that met at other times. These sub-groups in Corinth probably correspond in large part with the several prominent Christian people and households within cities, especially in Corinth. Paul speaks of the household of Stephanas in Corinth and insists on its prominence. Stephanas was one of the few Paul baptized (1 Cor 1:16; 16:15-16). Paul also mentions Crispus as one whom he baptized. The Acts describes the conversion of the whole house of Crispus (1 Cor 1:14; Acts 18:8). Acts likewise speaks of Aquila and Priscilla as well as Titius Justus. who at different times functioned as Paul's hosts (Acts 18:2-3. 7).

Evidence for a plurality of sub-groups within Corinth arises from the problem Paul addresses at the beginning of 1 Corinthians:

> I have been informed, my brothers, by certain members of Chloe's household that there are quarrels among you. I say this because each of you say, "I am of Paul; I am of Apollos; I am of Cephas." I, however, am of Christ. Is Christ divided? (1 Cor 1:11-13).

The divisions here are based on some form of alleged patronage. Whatever the nature of this divisiveness, the Corinthian church is clearly showing the strain of diverse groups within it. The existence of house churches within the city-wide church would go a long way to explain how such groups could arise.

A plurality of house churches appears in other cities addressed by Paul but not founded by Paul. In Rome we see the specific mention of the house church of Prisca and Aquila

(Rom 16:5), but we also see at least two other groups mentioned simply with a list of names along with "the brothers" or "the holy ones who are with them" (Rom 16:14-15).

In the Lycus valley of Asia we see a plurality of churches. Colossians 4:15 mentions the house church of Nympha in Laodicea while distinguishing this church from "the brothers" of the same city. If Philemon lived in Colossae—which is not certain—we would have a house church distinct from the group addressed by the letter to the Colossians. Philemon's house church would appear as a sub-group of that city church.

The picture of more than one house church within a city appears also in the descriptions of Antioch and Jerusalem. From these descriptions, however, we do not get a sense of strong local church unity. In Antioch at least two groups existed, between which Peter vacillated (Gal 2:11-13). These two groups show a pronounced closed character toward each other. Peter's joining the Jewish group meant his non-association with the Gentile group. Yet in Antioch Paul rebukes Peter "before all" (*emprosthen pantōn*, Gal 2:14). We are not informed about how and where the whole church of Antioch apparently met.

Acts describes a prayer gathering at the house of Mary, the mother of John Mark, which did not include "James and the brothers" (12:12-17). Since the family of John Mark, related to the Cypriot Barnabas, was probably a "Hellenist" family, this gathering may represent the house church of "the Hellenists," or Greek-speaking Jewish Christians, in Jerusalem (cf. Acts 6:1). Earlier Acts described a tension between the Hebrew-speaking and the Greek-speaking Christian in Jerusalem (6:1).

An exclusive and even hostile relationship marks the two house churches found in 3 John (vv. 6-10). On the one hand, we have Gaius whose household receives in open hospitality the emissaries of "the Elder" (vv. 1-8). On the other hand, we see Diotrephes who refuses such hospitality and even expels those in his church who would receive the emissaries of the Elder (vv. 9-10). In this letter there is no authority, other than the moral persuasion of the Elder, to counteract the division of the households.

The divisive character of many of these house churches may well explain why Paul concentrates on the city-wide church. While Paul affirms the existence of the private or single family house church, and while for Paul that house church remains the basic cell of the local church, he clearly wants those house churches to form a body with each other within the city-wide church. Instead of a group of house churches closed to each other or even hostile to each other, Paul envisions apparently a kind of federation of several house churches forming a local church. The Pauline local church existed thus on two levels, both connected with households, 1) a household assembly of an individual family and those associated with that family, and 2) a city-wide level meeting in a private home but consisting of several families.

Paul's emphasis on the city-wide meeting appears in a number of ways. The most obvious is his manner of addressing his letters to the whole church of a locality. He is the apostle and father to the whole church in a given city, and he addresses them as such.

He insists repeatedly on this local harmony and unity. A major section of 1 Corinthians deals with this theme (1:10-3:23; 12-14). He urges the Philippians to harmony:

> Make my joy complete by your union of thought, having the same love, united in soul, thinking the same way (2:2).

Taking a step to a wider perspective, he reminds the Colossians of the "joints and sinews" of the whole body by which true growth in mutual support can occur (2:19).

The letter to Philemon is the only exception to Paul's practice of addressing larger groups. This letter deals with the personal decision of one person. Nevertheless, it is directed to the wider group around Philemon.

Building up a local church on the basis of house churches would inevitably involve serious difficulties in keeping the house churches together. Any federation of Hellenistic households would contain a type of centrifugal force tending to destroy the unity of that federation. Family or household ties could involve intense loyalty. Ancient epitaphs eulogizing decreased members often express such sentiments of loyalty. According to Abraham Malherbe, the loyalty of the members to a household could rival even loyalty to the state.[7] In gathering the house churches together for a city-wide assembly and calling this city-wide assembly an *ekklēsia,* Paul most probably had in mind the city-wide assemblies of the Greek cities, assemblies called *ekklēsia.* This *ekklēsia* was the town meeting of the free citizens who gathered to decide matters affecting their welfare. These meetings appear from the 5th century B.C. on. The most well known of these *ekklēsiai* was that of Athens, which was the voting assembly of the free citizens. We find mention of such assemblies in other free cities of Greek constitution.[8] Although these assemblies had lost most of their power or in many cases simply ceased to exist in New Testament times, the use of the word for the lawful and unlawful meetings described in Acts 19:39.41 is evidence that something like these secular *ekklēsiai* continued to exist and be called such at the time of Paul.

5. Church as Gathering

The parallel between Paul's use of the term and the Greek municipal *ekklēsia* brings out another important aspect of the Pauline church. The Greek *ekklēsia* was an assembly. It came into existence and went out of existence as the citizens were gathered and dismissed. The emphasis of the word is on the gathering itself as an activity rather than on some permanent institution.

This meaning as "gathering" is clearest in the descriptions of "church" found in 1 Cor 11-14. A clear linguistic parallel ap-

---

[7]Abraham Malherbe, *Social Aspects of Early Christianity* (Baton Rouge: Louisiana State University, 1977), p. 69.

[8]Thucydides, *Histories,* 1:87.139; 6:8; 8:69; Philo, *On the Special Laws,* II, 44; *Every Good Man is Free,* 138; cf. Meeks, *Urban Christians,* p. 79.

pears between Paul's expressions, "When you assemble as church" (*en ekklēsia,* 11:18) and "when you assemble in the same place" (*epi to auto,* 11:20). Paul is speaking of the same event in both verses.

The instructions about the silence of women in 1 Cor 14:35 is expressed by the opposition between "at home" (*en oikō*) and "at church" (*en ekklēsia*). If we remember that the situation addressed by Paul (or perhaps a later editor) is taking place in a home, we might wonder what the problem is. On the other hand seeing the meaning of "church" here as "gathering," allows us to see the instructions as dealing with timing and an event, the moments of the Christians' gathering, rather than a special place.

Similarly when Paul contrasts the manner of eating appropriate for one's *oikia* and that for the *ekklēsia* (1 Cor 11:22), he seems to be dealing with different activities rather than different places.

In this section of 1 Corinthians, Paul repeatedly urges "building up the *ekklēsia*." This goal determines the proper use of the spiritual gifts (14:4.5.12; cf. 14:19.28). Again the admonition applies much more clearly to the actual gathering of the Christians than to any institutional existence of the same group. He is concerned about the orderly exercise of these gifts and their use in such a way that others can find some immediate benefit.

At times, however, Paul's meaning of the term *ekklēsia* drifts more to the group which assembles. This shading appears especially in the greetings where he addresses the Christians as a "church" (1 Cor 1:2; 2 Cor 1:1; 1 Thess 1:1, cf. Phil 4:15). Not far from the surface meaning in these instances, however, we can hear the note of the gathering. Paul applies the term to a group viewed as regularly meeting.

He never applies the term to refer, as we do today, to local assemblies seen as part of a larger unit. He never, of course, uses the term to refer to the building or the physical setting of the assembly, whether on the household level or on the city level. The physical setting of the assembly was a home, a building which functioned outside of "church time" as a private residence.

6. A World-wide Church?

The cohesiveness of the individual house churches into the local church arose for Paul because of a larger unifying context. This larger context gives hints of a world-wide perspective, a gathering that never gathers as such but which also bears the name "church."

When Paul refers to the Christians of a geographical area larger than the city, he does so usually by using the plural form, "churches." He refers to "the churches of Galatia" (1 Cor 16:1; Gal 1:2), "the churches of Asia" (1 Cor 16:19), "the churches of Macedonia" (2 Cor 8:1), and "the churches of Judea (Gal 1:22), or "the churches of God existing in Judea" (1 Thess 2:14). Paul also speaks about "the churches of the Gentiles" (Rom 16:4).

When referring to a teaching or rule observed universally by Christians, again Paul normally uses the plural form of "churches" or a distributive form which implies the plural. In "all the churches" or "every church" there are rules given (1 Cor 7:17), praise for Titus (2 Cor 8:18), things for Paul to worry about (2 Cor 11:28), and some common matter taught (1 Cor 4:17). Paul speaks of "all the churches of Christ" (Rom 16:16) or "all the churches of God" (1 Cor 11:16.22; cf. 2 Thess 1:4). "All the churches of the saints" likewise seems to include all Christians (1 Cor 14:33). Expressed here is concern for Christianity as larger than the locality, as a world-wide movement. But the term "church" here expresses the local or the domestic gathering and hence is used in the plural.

Nevertheless Paul at times uses the singular "the church" to designate what appears to be more than a local church. He writes, "God has appointed in the church first apostles, second prophets, then teachers . . ." (1 Cor 12:28). We have reference here to a generalized situation extending beyond Corinth and named simply as "the church" (cf. perhaps also 1 Cor 6:4).

It is particularly in Paul's expression "the church of God" that we hear resound a larger than local church. Paul uses this expression twice to name the Jewish Christians whom he persecuted (1 Cor 15:9; Gal 1:13; cf. Phil 3:6). In Galatians, he follows that expression by a reference to the "churches of

Judea" (1:22). Twice he calls the Corinthian believers "the church of God which is in Corinth" (1 Cor 1:2; 2 Cor 1:1). Paul also urges the Corinthians not to show contempt for "the church of God" by neglecting their fellow Corinthian Christians at the Lord's Supper (1 Cor 11:22). In these cases, the expression "church of God" is linked to a local group or set of groups. The ring of the expression, however, especially in the greeting to the Corinthians, sounds almost Platonic in its apparent dialectic of the universal and the particular. The larger reality is somehow realized and present in the particular.

When Paul admonishes the Corinthians not to give offense to "the church of God," we see a reference which clearly is meant to include all Christians:

> Give no offense to Jew or Greek or to the church of God,
> just as I try to please all in any way I can by seeking, not my
> own advantage, but that of the many (1 Cor 10:32-33).

In this case 'the church of God" stands parallel to "Jew or Greek" on the one side and "all" on the other.

What echoes in the background in Paul's use of "church" here is the Old Testament phrase *qehal yhwh*, "assembly of the Lord," translated by the Greek Bible as *ekklēsia tou kyriou*. This is the description of all the tribes of Israel gathered at Sinai by God to receive His law (Deut 23:2-4; cf. 9:10; 10:4). The expression *ekklēsia theou* occurs in the Greek Old Testament designating Israel as a whole people (Neh 13:1; cf. *ekklēsia hypsistou*, Sir 24:2).

The Sinai assembly, often designated as an *ekklēsia*, was of importance in late Judaism, the Jewish filter that passed the Old Testament to Paul and to the early Christian church. Philo used the term with this meaning several times.[9] The great assembly shows up in the writings of Qumran as the final

---

[9] *On the Virtues,* 108; *On Drunkenness,* 213; *On Dreams,* II.187; *Who is the Heir,* 251; *On the Decalogue,* 32.

or eschatological assembly, the final war, or a solemn meal with the anointed priest or prince.[10]

Paul pictures the Christians as the true Israel or at least as the new growth on the true Israel (Rom 9:6; 11:17) who by the Spirit have inherited the promises and the covenant (2 Cor 3:6). As the new children of Jerusalem (Gal 4:26-28), Christians are the people of God. Unlike the old Israel, however, Christians are not to think of ethnic limits. Christians could apply to themselves the international consciousness of Israel yet push it to even greater universality. Paul would thus expect the local church to have a real sense of belonging to a world-wide people.

Paul's world-wide concerns do not come to full expression in his use of the term "church." The concerns, however, consistently appear in the manner of his work and in other words and images in his letters. By the general manner of his work and writing, Paul reminds his readers of the larger movement to which they belong—without in any way organizing the churches so that one local church or church leader would have authority over another church.

We can find these concerns first of all in Paul's very apostolic work. His repeated visits, the visits of his associates, and his letters establish links among the local churches through himself. Furthermore, in his letters Paul often refers his local readers to the other churches. To the Romans he sends the greetings of "all the churches" (16:16). He greets the Corinthians "along with all who invoke the name of our Lord Jesus Christ in every place" (1 Cor 1:2) and compares his teaching for this church with "what I teach in every church" (4:17). The travels of local church members to other communities under the direction of Paul along with Paul's recommendations on behalf of these travelers suggests a more than casual network among the local churches (Rom 12:13; 16:1-2; 1 Cor 16:10-12; cf. Phil 2:25-30; Col 4:7-9; Eph 6:21-22).

The Christian community of Jerusalem, "the church of God"

---

[10] 1 QM 4:10; 1 QSa 2:3; cf. 1 QSa 1:25f; CD 7:17; 11:22; 12:6.

par excellence, functions for Paul as a reminder of the larger movement. The collection Paul takes up for the relief of "the poor" of Jerusalem (Rom 15:25-28; 1 Cor 16:1-4; 2 Cor 8-9) is for Paul a dramatic gesture acknowledging the central and unifying role of this church. Paul reminds the Gentile churches that they have shared in the spiritual goods of the Jerusalem church (Rom 15:27), even to the point of being secondary grafts onto the primary stock of the Jewish people (Rom 11:17). For Paul harmony with the Jerusalem church was a matter of not working in vain (Gal 2:2).

One might object that Paul had in mind a Gentile mission that was completely independent of the Jewish Christian mission. Gal 2:7-9 might sound like two separate and exclusive missions, one of Peter the other of Paul:

> Recognizing that I had been entrusted with the gospel for the uncircumcised, just as Peter was for the circumcised (for he who worked through Peter as his apostle among the Jews had been at work in me for the Gentiles) . . . they gave Barnabas and me the handclasp of fellowship, signifying that we should go to the Gentiles as they to the Jews.

Such an interpretation, however, runs contrary to Paul's work among Jewish Christians. "I became like a Jew for the Jews in order to gain the Jews" (1 Cor 9:20). The number of Jews in the Pauline churches, and perhaps even the descriptions throughout Acts of Paul preaching first in the Jewish synagogues, points out that this line was not just rhetoric.

The point of the accord in Jerusalem is, therefore, not that of exclusive apostolates. Rather the parallelism in this accord simply underlines the equality of the missions. As Peter has his mission, so Paul has his.

The food restrictions maintained by the Jewish Christians posed serious problems for the interaction of Jew and Gentile believers, particularly in the celebration of the Lord's Supper. But Paul never saw the two groups as forming two separate churches. Gentiles were one with the Jerusalem church and indebted to them for a spiritual heritage (Rom 9-11).

Jerusalem, however, never functioned for the Pauline churches as a sort of super-church. The agreement Paul works out with the "eminent leaders" (*hoi dokountes*) of this church is not some legal edict to be obeyed, but an agreement among equals sealed by a handshake (Gal 2:9). Paul insists on his personal independence from the apostles "before him" (Gal 1:17.19).

A far more important indication of a universal dimension to Paul's work is his way of speaking about Christians and the local churches as "the body of Christ." Urging the Corinthians to allow the diverse gifts of the community to cohere in harmonious effort, Paul writes, "You are the body of Christ. Each one is a member" (1 Cor 12:27). Paul is urging the unity of life in a local church, but he does so by reminding the Corinthians that they are more than a local church. They must live in harmony because they are the body of Christ, not a part of the body, but the whole—just as they are "the church of God."

Again dealing with the same topic, he writes almost the same thing to the Romans, "We are one body in Christ, members of one another" (12:5). With the first person plural Paul includes himself and all his churches in this unity of Christ.

The role of Christ in this metaphor is left vague. If anything Christ appears as the whole unity. The Spirit is a special medium or power assuring this in-corporation into Christ. "It was in one Spirit that all of us, whether Jew or Greek, slave or free, were baptized into one body. All of us have been watered by the one Spirit" (1 Cor 12:13).

In Colossians the theme of "the body of Christ" reappears and is explicitly identified with "the church," now clearly understood as a larger than local reality. Christ's relationship shifts to that of "head."

> It is he who is head of the body, the church (1:18).
> In my own flesh I fill up what is lacking in the sufferings of Christ for his body which is the church (1:24).

The metaphor functions now more to insist on unity and growth rather than the interdependence of the members. "The whole body supported and strengthened by joints and sinews grows with the growth of God" (2:19).

Colossians stands out from the other letters of Paul likewise in the heavenly and cosmic colors with which it pictures this "universal church." The letter focuses on the victorious and cosmic Christ into whose kingdom of light believers have already entered (1:9-2:7). The theology of Colossians is developed from the view of the resurrection as already occurring.

> By baptism you are buried with Christ, in whom you are already raised" (2:12; compare Rom 6:5).

This realized eschatology leads to a heavenly perspective for Christian morality.

> If you have been raised with Christ, seek the things above where Christ is seated at the right hand of God" (3:1).

If the church is Christ's body, then the church would share this heavenly and cosmic existence of its head. This "more than local" church then is not a world-wide organization or network of local groups seeking to be an assembly of God in the world, it is rather the heavenly kingdom itself, now hidden in Christ but to be revealed with him.

Are these ideas really new in Paul? The stress in Colossians on the universal character of the church is new, but the roots of the idea can be found in the earlier letters, as we have seen. The earlier Pauline picture of this "more than local" church, however, is much more earthy in some parallel to Israel as a world-wide people. The "anagogic," however, is not totally lacking in earlier Paul. Writing to the Galatians he contrasted the people of the Christian faith with that of the Jewish in terms of "the Jerusalem above" (*hē anō Ierousalēm*) and the "the now Jerusalem" (*hē nyn Ierousalēm*, 4:25-26). He reminds the Philippians of "our commonwealth (*politeuma*) in heaven" (3:20).

The arguments against seeing Paul as the author of Colossians rest heavily on the shifts in theology found in this letter when compared to the earlier letters. Although these shifts are important, they are not without earlier hints in Paul, as is clear with the Colossian picture of the universal church. The arguments concerning the authorship of Colossians based on theological shifts therefore remain unsure. Was this letter written under the supervision of Paul? If so then we see the final development of his thought. If not, then a follower of Paul took an important step beyond Paul, but one organically coherent with Paul's earlier thought.

2

Background in the Hellenistic World

While we translate the expressions of Paul, *oikos, oikia,* with terms meaningful to us, "house, home, household," we must be careful not to read into Paul's statements the meanings which the English words have for us. Words change with each generation and sometimes with each writer. What Paul meant by the "house church" depended on the Hellenistic culture of his time, with both its Gentile and Jewish components.

1. The Household

The two words Paul uses, *oikos* and *oikia,* from which we derive the English, "economy" and "economics," meant roughly the same, namely, the household with its persons and property. Classical Greek maintained some distinction between the two words, whereby *oikos* brought to mind especially the idea of wealth, possessions, or a physical room whereas *oikia* suggested more the relatives, servants, or even clients of a household. Both words were used for the dwelling, the family, or the kin.

Paul's Greek, however, shows much more affinity to the Greek of the Septuagint, the 2nd century BC translation of the Hebrew and Aramaic Old Testament made for Greek-speaking Jews like Paul himself. The translators of the Septuagint needed to translate the Hebrew word *bait,* which at times meant a room in a building (Est 2:3; 7:8); the whole family, including father (Gen 50:8; 1 Sam 1:21), wife, second wife, sons, daughters (Gen 36:60), dependent relatives (Gen 13:1), servants (Gen 15:2-3), attendants (Gen 14:14), and slaves (Gen 17:13.27); relatives who formed a group between the immediate family and the tribe (2 Sam 9:7); along with household possessions, including wealth, tools, slaves, and cattle (Ex 20:17; Est 8:1). Without any apparent distinction, these translators chose both *oikos* and *oikia* to express the broad concept of *bait*. The only perceived difference between the two Greek words is the greater frequency of *oikos* over *oikia*.

Considered from either its Hellenistic or its Jewish roots, the concept of the *oikos* is thus considerably larger than our concept of "family." Even the word "household" in our vocabulary does not do justice to the extension of the Jewish/ Hellenistic concept.

A comment by Cicero about one's hierarchy of duties reflects his understanding of a "household." Our duties, according to the Roman orator and poet, begin with one's country, then one's parents, "next come children and the whole household (*domus*), who look to us alone for support and can have no other protection; finally our kinsmen."[1] Besides one's immediate family, Cicero has in mind unattached relatives, slaves, freedmen, hired workers, sometimes tenants, business partners and clients.

Cicero defines the *domus* or household by a relationship of dependence, not kinship. In fact the family or household was constituted by the reciprocal relationships of protection and subordination. At the top of the pyramid was the *paterfamilias,* the family father or other "head of the house," whose power extended at times to that of the children's life or death. At the bottom of the structure was the slave, who nevertheless could exercise considerable responsibility in his household duties. Supporting this authority was the subordination of the members of the household who by this subordination enjoyed a

[1] *De Officiis,* 1,17,58.

sense of belonging and security not provided by any other social or political structure of the time.

Were all the members of a household expected to share the same religious practices? Although our information about this expectation is scarce, we can probably presume that all members, especially those of the smaller households, felt some pressure to share in the household cults (the *lares*). Yet the religious solidarity characteristic of the old agrarian society gave way under the pressures of urbanization. In imperial times, Romans became more laissez-faire about the religion of their slaves. This latitude regarding religion appears in the strongly Romanized cities more so than in the Greek East.[2]

Ancient sources speak of the household as the basic political and economic unit and basis of society.[3] The family was supposed to be a microcosm of the state or *politeia*. The head of the family mirrored the king. Thus any person with political ambitions would first have to prove his ruling capacity in the family,[4] a thought reflected in the Pastoral Epistles about the proving ground of a bishop.

2. Ancient Homes

It is important to have a sense of the physical buildings that housed the families of the ancient world. Archeology is guide in this matter.

The very floor plans of the wealthier homes in Pompeii and on the island of Delos tell us something of the relationships within the family. Here we see private rooms and offices for the head of the house. The women and the children are relegated to a special section of the house as are the slaves. Many houses seem to have rooms for rent and a shop or two along the street. Most important is the dining room where the

[2]cf. Meeks, *Urban Christians*, p. 30, and n. 139.
[3]Aristotle, *Politics* 1252 b 9-19; cf. also Plutarch, *Life of Lycurgus* 19,3.
[4]Sophocles, *Antigone*, 661f.

paterfamilias could entertain his peers, clients, and friends from other households.[5]

The size and shape of these villas is important for estimating the size of both the private and the city-wide house church. Jerome Murphy-O'Connor has collected the archeological data on a number of first century villas in and away from Corinth.[6] Most of these homes took the shape of a Roman atrium house, a series of rooms facing each other around a courtyard with a small pool. The Villa at Anaploga, near Corinth, contained a dining room or *triclinium* that measured 5.5 by 7.5 meters, or 41.25 square meters (cf. figure 1). Such a room would allow nine people to recline on couches around the wall. The *atrium,* where possibly guests might overflow, measured 5 by 6 meters, with about 1/9th of that area occupied by the pool.

These dimensions seem fairly representative. A villa at Pompeii, destroyed in AD 79 shows a somewhat smaller *triclinium,* 4 by 6.3 meters, and an atrium 7 by 6 meters (cf. figure 2). Some three hundred years later a villa was built at Olynthus, Greece, southeast of Thessalonica with almost the same size *triclinium,* 5.8 by 5 meters, but a much larger atrium, measuring 10 by 10 meters (cf. figure 3). Another house near the Sicyonian gate at Corinth, described by the excavator as a "sumptuous villa" had a somewhat larger *triclinium,* about 7 by 7 meters. The atrium was almost the same size. This villa was from the 2nd century, rebuilt on an earlier house.

If we averaged out these sizes, we would arrive at a villa with a *triclinium* of some 36 square meters and an *atrium* of 55 square meters. If we removed all the couches from the *triclinium,* we would end up with space for perhaps 20 persons. If we included the atrium, minus any large decorative urns, we could expand the group to perhaps 50 persons, provided

[5]cf. Meeks, *Urban Christians,* p. 30 and n. 136 for references.

[6]*St. Paul's Corinth. Texts and Archaeology* (Wilmington, DE: Glazier, 1983), p. 155.

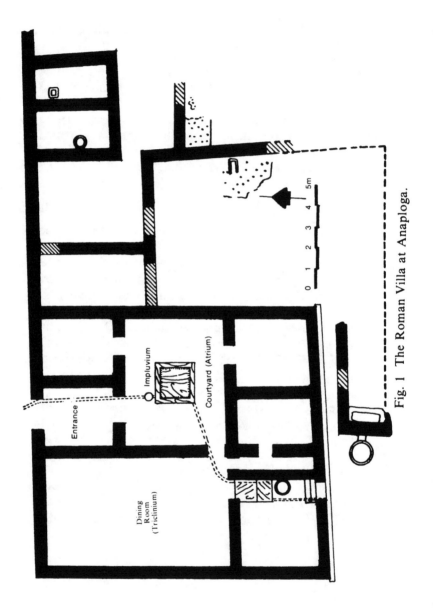

Fig. 1 The Roman Villa at Anaploga.

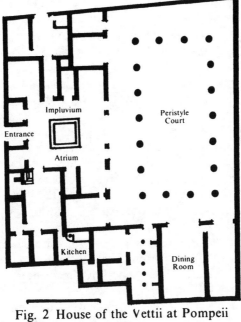

Fig. 2 House of the Vettii at Pompeii

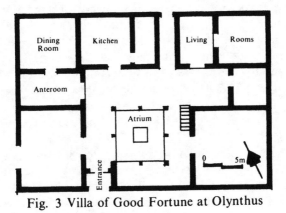

Fig. 3 Villa of Good Fortune at Olynthus

people did not move around, and some did not mind getting shoved into the shallow pool. The maximum comfortable group such a villa could accommodate would most likely be in the range of 30 to 40 persons.

3. *The Economic Stratification of Society*

Thus far we glimpse at the wealthier households—since wealth tends to leave testimonies to itself. Harder to envision are the poorer households. Roman society was intensely vertical. Property ownership, the single most important sign of wealth in the Roman world, was concentrated in the hands of a small percentage of the population. The highest levels of aristocracy, the senators and equites of the empire along with the municipal decurions, comprised slightly more than 1/10 of one percent of the population. These were the owners of vast estates in the countryside, palaces for residences, and large rental property for income.

About three percent of the population of Rome lived in one-third of the residential space of the city. The masses were crowded into hugh tenements, called *insulae*. The common apartment (*cenaculum*) of an *insula* rented for about 40 denarii a month. Since a denarius was generally a common laborer's daily wage, poorer families had to band together and share these small living quarters. By contrast a spacious *domus* on the ground floor of an *insula* rented for about 625 denarii a month. After the fire, Nero had encouraged the Italian decurions to display their wealth by rebuilding houses in Rome worth at least 25,000 denarii. In this "Manhattan on the Tiber," being a house owner with a comfortable dining room to entertain a small group of co-religionists meant being a very wealthy persons.

Rome was perhaps more expensive to live in than other cities, yet Rome was not untypical. In Egypt a house in ruins sold for 2,000 silver drachmae. The Greek drachma was equivalent to a Roman denarius. At the other end of the scale, an estate with villa and land rented for 1 talent, 4,000 drachmae a year. The talent was equivalent to 6,000 drachmae.[7]

Due to the cost of housing, the average population density in the cities of the Empire was about 200 persons per acre. That ratio is the equivalent density of the industrial slums in modern Western cities. To alleviate this misery, municipalities generally dedicated about one fourth of the city to public areas. The attractive spaciousness of these public facilities allowed the bulk of the population to put up with the uncomfortable crowding at home. Once we move, then, from the circle of the rich to that of the poor we must envision life with little privacy, lived on the streets, sidewalks, and squares.

This economic information is important for the understanding of house churches. From it we see the relatively high social status of the heads of the house churches, especially those who hosted city-wide assemblies. If Gaius of Corinth had a house with a room large enough for all the Corinthian Christians, he must have been a wealthy man. Furthermore, it is difficult to see how a poor person of Corinth or Rome could have hosted any assembly, even that of an individual household.

4. Religion in the Home

Religion was a normal part of the Hellenistic household long before the Christians met at a house church. For the pagan household, the house cult was an explicit expression of religiosity in the home. These cults took place within the confines and in the privacy of the home. In the Roman cults, the father of the house was the head of the cult without any external confirmation.

Among the gods venerated in the house cults were Hestia,

[7]References in Lloyd Michael White, *Domus Ecclesia—Domus Dei. Adaptation and Development in the Setting for Early Christian Assembly,* Ph.D. dissertation, Yale University, 1982, pp. 545-553.

goddess of the hearth. The occasions for the exercise of these house cults were generally the special days in the life of a family—birthdays, marriages, deaths, coming of age rites, and memorials of the dead. Toasts at the end of meals or at the beginning of symposia likewise alluded to the household gods.

Because of their private character and because they left little documentation behind, these cults are generally neglected in modern studies. Yet this religious practice may very well have marked the daily life of individuals far more than did any public cult. Cicero describes the sanctity of the home itself in terms of these household cults:

> What is holier, what is better made secure by any religion than the house of each citizen? Here are the altars; here the hearth, here the household gods, here the sacred, the religious, and the ceremonies together.This refuge is thus so sacred to all that no one has the right to break in.[8]

On the other hand, Plato expressed a negative reaction to the sanctuaries in the house:

> No man shall have sacred rites in a private house. When he would sacrifice, let him go to the temples and hand over his offerings to the priests and priestesses, who see to the sanctity of such things.... The reason of this is as follows:— Gods and temples are not easily instituted, and to establish them rightly is the work of a mighty intellect.

Plato complains particularly of women "who have a way of consecrating the occasion, vowing sacrifices, and promising shrines to Gods" (*Laws,* 909-910). This minority position of Plato fits into his general bias against the private life and his disdain of the common person. His fear of the unregulated religion and his suspicions against women in particular, however, show up again in the Pastoral Epistles of the New Testament.

[8] *De Domo Sua,* 41,104.

5. The Jewish Household

Where household religiosity dominated and where we find the closest background to the Christian house church is in the Jewish household. In the Jewish world at the time of the New Testament, the family was the primary place for the transmission of the faith. The family prayed daily in common mornings and evenings and especially at the blessings of the mealtime. Among the religious feasts celebrated at home were New Years, Atonement, Sukkot with its building in the gardens of the house, Shavuot (the Feasts of Weeks) with its decorating of the house with flowers, Hanukkah, and Purim.

The pre-eminent family feast was the celebration of Passover. This feast was the high point of the year and during New Testament times was held in the homes. As Philo wrote concerning Passover, "Each house at this time took on the character of the holiness of the Temple."[9] We still know very little about the life of the ancient Jewish household with its multiplicity of customs and its inner piety. This silence and privacy concerning the Jewish home, however, was its strongest asset. Whenever external difficulties threatened the public practice of Jewish worship, the Jewish home could assume full responsibility for the practice of religion. As long as the Jewish household maintained itself, Judaism as a religion was protected from any threat.

A Jewish group who have shed great light on the New Testament are the Essenes. Their writings have provided expressions and practices in striking parallel to the early Christians. We know this group mostly from the documents left near a monastic type of community on the banks of the Dead Sea in what are now the ruins of Qumran. At Qumran the term "house" was used frequently to designate the community,[10] much the way the Old Testament spoke of Israel as a

[9] *On the Special Laws,* II, 145,148.
[10] 1 QS 5:6; 8:9; 9:65.

house. The ancient Jewish writers, Josephus and Philo, however, tell of communities of Essenes throughout Palestine numbering as many as 4,000.[11] These Essenes outside of Qumran apparently lived and assembled in private homes. Josephus refers to a "house" where they met for meals and instructions.[12] Philo refers to them sharing their houses.[13] Such home-based communities would be close parallels to the Christian house churches.

6. *Hellenistic Private Cults and Social Associations*

The local church had an important parallel in the Hellenistic clubs and cults at the time of the New Testament, which existed in the ever widening social space between the individual households order (*oikonomiae*) and the public life of the state (*politeia*).

These voluntary associations (*koinōniae*) filled an important vacuum in Greco-Roman life. As political power was concentrated in the hands of fewer and fewer for longer periods of time, many citizens experienced a general disenchantment with the *polis*. The alternative to simply closing oneself in one's *oikos,* was to become involved with some voluntary and private association.

Some of these associations were fundamentally cultic, like the orders of Dionysus or those of Mithras, the Persian bull-slayer. Others were predominantly social, like the trade guilds (*collegia*) which met mostly to have a meal and drink some good wine. Almost all these groups, however, contained an important religious dimension, particularly that of providing a decent burial for their members.

Despite periodic attempts by the government to suppress

---

[11]cf. Philo, *Every Good Man is Free,* 75f; *Hypothetica* 11.1; Josephus, *Jewish Antiquities* 18:10; *Jewish War* II, 124.

[12]*Jewish War* II, 129.132.

[13]*Every Good Man is Free,* 85; *Hypothetica,* 11,4; cf. Josephus *Jewish War* II, 122.

them, these cults and associations proliferated in imperial times. Their formation was relatively simple. A group, usually ranging from twelve to fifty, would gather (*synagein*), draw up a constitution, find a meeting place, and declare themselves to be "The Association of N."
Some groups like those of the cult of Mithras had no connection with households—except to exclude women from participation. Most others formed around households. As cults these associations existed between the private house-cults and the public religion. The meetings of these associations and their ceremonies took place in private houses, but they included more than one family. They became, as it were, a community around a family.
The most challenging part of getting started was finding a meeting place. Getting a house in which to meet was one of the primary concerns of a new association. Preserved as important memories therefore are the actions of philosophers bequeathing their houses and lands to their philosophical schools[14] or of founders of cults establishing sanctuaries in their homes.[15] Although many of these establishments involve a dedicated sanctuary, examples exist of houses which were used for cultic purposes only from time to time and otherwise were private dwellings.[16]
The one providing such a meeting place became the group's patron and usually received high honors from the group. As numerous inscriptions indicate, the very name of the association often included the patron's name, like 'The Association in the Home of Sergia Paullina.'"[17] Because of the crucial

[14]For references cf. Klauck, *Hausgemeinde*, p. 87, esp. n. 26, 27.

[15]cf. Martin Nilsson, *Geschichte der griechischen Religion* (2nd ed., 2 vols; Munich: Beck: 1961), II, 291; S.C. Barton & G.H.R. Horseley, "A Hellenistic Cult Group and the New Testament Churches," *Jahrbuch fuer Antike und Christentum*, 24 (1981), 7-14.

[16]Cf. the cult of Orgeones in Athens. References in Klauck, *Hausgemeinde*, p. 86-87.

[17]*Corpus Inscriptionum Latinarum*, (Berlin: 1863-1909), 6.9148; other examples in Jean Waltzing, *Etude sur les corporations professionelles chez les Romains* (4 vols.; Louvain: Peeters, 1895-1900), III, 222-264.

dependence of the group on his or her good will, the patron of the club generally held effective control of the club's life.

Under the umbrella of the patron a club would often function under the semblance of democratic governance, imitating the classical *polis* in organization and decision-making procedures.[18] Titles imitated the titles of municipal officials: *magistri, quaestores, decuriones, quinquennales,* and *curatores* in Roman clubs; *logistai, grammateis, epistatai, archontes, prytaneis,* and *hegemones* among many other offices in the Greek counterparts.

An interesting example of a voluntary association is the Dionysian association, or *thiasos,* founded by Pompeia Agrippinilla. We have what appears to be the membership list of this club, with some 400 names. Pompeia is listed first as the priestess and head of the club. Next come the members of her immediate family, also with sacral offices: the husband, the children, the relatives, clients, servants and slaves in that order. The household hierarchy obviously continued to function in the club. Some senatorial families appear on the list. Further down the list, apparently indicating less importance, are more Greek names.[19]

With the exception of the Dionysian clubs, most of these voluntary associations tended to be homogeneous in the social status of their members. The wealthy joined the clubs of the rich. The military associated with military. Tradesmen formed guilds with others in their profession. The cults of Dionysus, on the other hand, provided opportunities for slaves and senators to hob-nob. However, the slaves of this club were the slaves of the wealthy in the same club. This was not an abandonment of classes. Rather, the social hierarchy of the family was reproduced within the club.

The analogies between these Hellenistic clubs and the early church are striking. We are not surprised by the fact that the common term for such clubs, *thiasos,* was applied to Christian

[18]Meeks, *Urban Christians,* p. 78.

[19]Cf. Meeks, p. 31 & n. 143.

groups of the second century, by both non-Christians[20] and Christians.[21]

It would not appear, however, that Christian groups consciously modeled themselves on these clubs. With the exception perhaps of the title *episcopos,* the titles and terminology the club members used for themselves and their leaders is completely absent in the New Testament. Paul uses the technical verb *synagein* one time (1 Cor 5:4), but to describe the meeting of the Christians, not their foundation as a group. The intensity of commitment made by Christians to their movement, the involvement of being "baptized into Christ Jesus" (Rom 6:3), is unparalleled in Hellenistic associations.

Nevertheless we should not underestimate the more or less spontaneous and diffused influence of these associations on the early Christians. Luke describes Paul in dramatic contact with these associations, in conflict with the Artemis guild in Ephesus (Acts 19:24-27), preaching to the philosophers of Athens (Acts 17:18), using the hall of Tyrannus in Ephesus (Acts 19:9). While these descriptions perhaps say more about Luke than about Paul, the echoes and references of philosophical teachings found in Paul's own writings (1 Cor 1:20; 2:45; 15:33; cf. Acts 17:28) as well as the explicit injunctions of Paul against aspects of these cults (1 Cor 8:7-13; 10:14-22) indicate his familiarity with the currents of his culture.

7. Women in the Hellenistic World

Because of the conspicuous presence of women in connection with the Pauline house church, we need to see more carefully the role of women in the Greco-Roman household and society.

Musonius Rufus speaks of the traditional role of married

---

[20]Celsus according to Origen, *Against Celsus,* III, 23.

[21]Tertullian, *Apology,* 39; cf. J. Weiss, who summarizes earlier discussions on this matter, *Der erste Korintherbrief* (9th ed.; Goettingen: Vandenhoeck & Ruprecht, 1910), xx-xxix.

women, the management of the household, the direction of the affairs within the confines of the house. Departing from tradition Musonius uses this role as the basis to argue that women should study philosophy and that daughters should, except for vocational training, receive the same education as sons.[22]

Outside the home some limited opportunities existed for women. A small but significant number of women's names can be found on coins and inscriptions indicating them as recipients of municipal honors, mostly because of their role as benefactors.[23] Traditionally women were disqualified from political life. But again in what appears to be a realistic portrayal, Aristophanes describes married women attending civic speeches and religious rituals, as well as shopping and publicly moving about without special constraints.[24]

We see women active in commerce and manufacturing, especially in luxury goods like purple dye and perfume. Acts 16:14 describes Lydia as a business woman, traveling freely. The description appears representative of at least widows of business men in Macedonia. A brief mention in the Mishnah describes women assisting their husbands in their craft or profession, in sales as well as in production.[25] This description stands in contrast to the rigid mysogynism of other texts, which scholars now see as reflecting later Judaism more than New Testament times.

Apparently wider opportunities existed for women outside of Greece. In the East and especially in Rome, noblewomen were able to move about freely in public, receive some education, and belong to women's societies.[26] As described by

---

[22]For text and discussion cf. Cora Lutz, "Musonius Rufus: 'The Roman Socrates,'" *Yale Classical Studies,* 10 (1947), 3-147.

[23]Ramsay MacMullen "Women in Public in the Roman Empire," *Historia,* 29 (1980), 208-218.

[24]*Frogs,* 1346-51.

[25]*Ketuboth,* 9:4.

[26]Cf. Livy, *Ab Urbe condita,* III, 44ff; Pliny, *Epistulae,* IV, 19:1-5; Ovid, *Ars amatoria,* III, 634-42.

Sallust[27] and Tacitus,[28] some women indirectly exerted considerable influence in political affairs.

Unmarried daughters were rigidly restricted both in Jewish and Gentile circles. Philo speaks about restricting the girls of the house to limited quarters within the confines of the house.[29] Marriage, however, came early in the life of a girl.

In the inscriptions from the Hellenistic associations, women appear alongside of men, usually in much smaller proportions. In Greece, women appear more frequently in groups related to the goddess Artemis. Outside Greece the feminine names are mostly in family associations.[30]

Wealthy women, especially those who made money from commerce, were fairly often asked to serve as founders or patrons of men's clubs. In Italy and in the Latin-speaking provinces, about one-tenth of the protectors and donors of *collegia* were women.[31] Such a role meant providing a place of meeting in her home or in a special building. In addition the role often involved providing an endowment for the expenses of the club.

Ancient cults of various kinds had priestesses. Literature of the time characterizes women as drawn especially to the syncretic cults of Egypt and the East. Apuleius describes a prominence of women in the cult of Isis.[32] Juvenal's sixth satire blames the lush growth of these cults on the superstition and irresponsibility of emancipated women.[33] However, the inscriptions do not support the view that women were the leaders in religious innovations. In private family cults, however, women do appear at times as the priestess or leader.[34]

---

[27] *Bellum Catilinae*, XXIV, 3; XXV, 5.

[28] *Annales*, 1:3-14.

[29] *Flaccus*, II, 89.

[30] Cf. Meeks, *Urban Christians*, p. 23-25.

[31] Cf. MacMullin, "Women in Public," p. 211.

[32] *The Golden Ass*, XI, 6ff.

[33] *Satire VI*, esp. 511-592.

[34] Meeks, *Urban Christians*, p. 25.

When the gospels describe women following Jesus (Lk 8:1-3; Matt 20:20), entertaining visiting teachers and listening to instruction (Lk 10:38-42; 11:27-28; Jn 11:20; 12:2), these texts appear to be reflecting the norms of the time. They do not present these practices as surprising or as some special innovation by Jesus.

On the other hand the gospels give evidence of the norm restricting a woman from conversing with a stranger (Lk 1:39-40; 8:19-21, 43; Jn 4:7), a practice that Jesus may well have deliberately violated. This prevailing norm is perhaps understood better in the light of a practice, described by Sallust, of courtesans (*hetairai*) engaging in public discussions with men.[35]

8. The Jewish Synagogue

The influence of Hellenistic associations on the early Christians may have occurred through a Jewish institution that by far shows the closest parallels to the Christian *ekklēsia*, namely, the Jewish synagogue. Recent studies have detected very specific influence of the Hellenistic associations on Jewish counterparts.[36]

The origins of the Jewish synagogue remain obscure and are generally thought to be rooted in the Babylonian exile experience.[37] The earliest inscriptions evidence their existence from the 3rd century BC. In New Testament times, we have the references in the gospels to the Galilean synagogues (Matt 4:23; 9:35; Lk 4:15, etc.). Philo refers to diaspora synagogues as "prayer houses."[38]

The meaning of the word "synagogue" shows the same shift

---

[35] *Bellum Catilinae*, XXIII, 3-4; XXVII, 2.

[36] Cf. H. Dombrowski, "*yahad* in 1 QS and *to koinon*: An Instance of Early Greek and Jewish Synthesis," *Harvard Theological Review*, 59 (1966), 293-307; M. Hengel, *Judaism and Hellenism;* trans. J. Bowden 2 vols; Philadelphia, 1974), I, 243ff.

[37] Cf. I. Sonne, "Synagogue," *Interpreters Dictionary of the Bible*, IV, 477ff.

[38] *On the Embassy to Gaius*, 156, 311; *Moses*, II, 215; *Flaccus*, 45.

that the term "church" eventually undergoes. In its earliest meaning the word referred to the gathering. The Greek, *synagōgē*, is simply a noun form from the verb, *synagein*, meaning "to gather." We see this active meaning in Acts 13:43. Later the term is applied to the group that meets (cf. Acts 6:9; 9:2; Rev 2:9; 3:9). Finally by association, the word names the building in which the group meets (Matt 4:23; 9:35; 13:54; Acts 13-19 *passim*, etc.).

For our study it is important to see the connection between the synagogue and the private house. That connection as well as the development of that connection seems parallel to the Christian church.

Four 3rd century A.D. synagogues and one 1st century B.C. synagogue have been the focus of recent study.[39] These five synagogues show the same type of development, all from private dwellings.

The earliest is that of the island of Delos, off the coast of Greece. It appears to be a synagogue created from a private home presumably with a peristyle. The renovation consisted of the construction of interior partition walls to create a simple rectangular hall. Nothing otherwise seems to distinguish the building from the neighboring residences. Some inscriptions and the general form of the meeting hall suggests that the Jews of Delos already functioned in the form of an ethnic *thiasos* at the time of the renovations. It could very well be, then, that the private house prior to its renovations was used by the Delos Jews for community purposes.

The 3rd century A.D. synagogues similarly appear to be renovations of private houses. The one uncovered at Priene, now in western Turkey, developed from an upper-class city house. The renovation of the third century created an assembly room, 10 by 13 meters. Other living quarters were not destroyed but probably assumed community functions as guest chambers, caretaker's quarters, or a school. The renovation looks like the work of a developed community. Adjacent

---

[39]Cf. White, *Domus Ecclesiae*, pp. 248-378, 437-474.

houses including street front structures are affected. Therefore
we again are faced with the possibility of the use of the pre-
existing home for religious purposes prior to these extensive
renovations.

A third century synagogue in Ostia Antica, Italy, was built
on a peristyle house of the 1st century A.D., which was already
used as a synagogue. An inscription from the site reads, "Mindis
Faustus constructed [the synagogue] and made it from his
own rooms."[40]

At Stobi of Macedonia archeologists uncovered a Christian
basilica built on the foundation of two prior synagogues, the
oldest of which was developed from a private villa. An inscription associated with the first synagogue reads:

> I Claudius Tiberius Polycharmos ... Father of the Syn-
> agogue at Stobi, having lived my whole life according to
> Judaism, in accordance with a vow, [gave] the [my] houses
> to the holy place (*tō hagiō topō*), along with the *triclinium*
> and its *tetrastoa*, out of my household accounts.... How-
> ever [I retain] ownership and disposition of all the upper
> chambers for myself (*tēn exousia tōn hyperōōn*).[41]

Here we have a clear example of a patron's role in the erection
of a synagogue. Polycharmos, a wealthy man, dedicates his
house as an act of devotion. In turn he receives a position of
honor in the synagogue as "Father of the Synagogue." Most
interesting for our study is the founder's desire and right to
continue to live in the building, at least in certain rooms of the
building.

In Dura-Europos, in eastern Syria, excavators uncovered a
synagogue not far from a Christian house transformed into a
church. The synagogue appears to have gone through three
stages of development. From roughly AD 50-150 it was a

---

[40]Text in White, *Domus Ecclesiae*, p. 326.
[41]Text from White, *Domus Ecclesiae*, pp. 302-304.

private house. Around AD 165 it was renovated to function as a synagogue. The renovation maintained the basic architecture of the private house, with a central court and rooms around the court including a dining room and the main assembly room, roughly 11 by 5 meters. The meeting room was described by Carl Kraeling, the director of the project, as:

> an oversize version of a room of a private house.... It represents the private house, the natural locus for the development of a congregational group, adapted by a minimum of changes to meet the needs of the group in worship.[42]

At roughly AD 200 the synagogue was rebuilt with a larger assembly hall (13.65 by 7.68 meters). The other rooms of the structure were eliminated to provide a large court yard. This building was destroyed in AD 256. At least during its second stage, part of the building was continually lived in.

In these five buildings, the earliest synagogues uncovered by archeology, we have the same pattern of a Jewish community beginning with a private home, probably using that home for religious purposes, then at a particular point renovating the home to develop a special assembly area, and finally redoing the whole building to build a dedicated synagogue. Although we know synagogues were plentiful in periods earlier than these buildings, we have little archeological evidence of them. Of course, if these earlier synagogues were private homes, they would be architecturally indistinguishable and would thus leave no trace for archeologists.

9. Larger Jewish Networks and Institutions

The Jews of ancient Sardis stand out from other contemporary Jewish communities in two ways. First, the synagogue

---

[42]Kraeling, *The Synagogue. The Excavations at Dura-Europos. Final Report,* Vol 8, pt. 1 (New Haven: Yale University, 1956), pp. 22 & 33.

of this community, uncovered by recent excavations and dating from either the late 2nd or early 3rd century A.D., was from the beginning a monumental building, not a private house. A large hall somewhat in the form of a basilica, the building apparently was constructed by the city for public purposes and then sold to the Jewish community. With assets large enough to purchase a large public building, this community must have had an earlier synagogue in the city, one which again has left no trace for archeologists. Perhaps the earlier synagogue was of a more private type.

Secondly, this community stands out by the clear record of its officially recognized and city-wide organization. Josephus relates the decree of Lucius Antonius (49 BC) sent to the magistrates, council and *dēmos* of Sardis recognizing the Jewish organization or *synodos:*

> Jewish citizens of ours have come to me and pointed out that from the earliest times they have had an association [*synodos*] of their own in accordance with their native laws and a place [*topos*] of their own, in which they decide their affairs and controversies with one another.[43]

Josephus also relates the corresponding decree of the council and *dēmos* of Sardis, confirming the rights of Jewish citizens of Sardia

> to come together and have a communal life [*politeuesthai*] and adjudicate suits among themselves, and that a place be given them in which they may gather together with their wives and children and offer their ancestral prayers and sacrifices to God.[44]

The Jewish community of Sardis was not alone in forming a city-wide community. Both Philo and Josephus tell us of a

[43]*Jewish Antiquities* 235.

[44]*Jewish Antiquities* 259-61.

council of elders in Alexandria, a council of elders who represented the Jewish community in negotiations with city officials.[45] In the first century the Jews of Antioch were all associated under one *archōn.*[46]

Like the Gentile associations, the Jewish groups had offices and titles parallel to those of the municipality. The most regular office that appears is that of *archōn,* "leader." We also hear of the *grammateus* or "secretary" and of a *decania,* a council of ten leaders, functioning as head of a synagogue.

These Jewish associations give us the closest parallels to the early Christian churches. Like the churches, the Jewish synagogues were rooted in the private house, forming most probably an extended family, expanding the basic religious character of the Jewish household. But like the churches of Paul, the Jewish synagogue becomes much larger than the family and in many cases, a city-wide association.

Like the Christian churches, the Jewish synagogues belonged to a larger entity, Israel, the People of God, represented concretely by the city of Jerusalem and its Temple. This worldwide entity existed without any structure or legal institution binding the diaspora communities together. The world-wide entity was an extension and projection of the life of the local community with its sense of being the People of God.[47]

On all three dimensions, then, the household, the locality, and the world, we see parallels to the early Christian sense of "gathering." For both Jews and Christians, religious life was a complex of three concentric circles, beginning in the family and extending to the world. The wider circle depended for its identity and vitality on the next smaller, so that eventually the household gathering functioned as foundation of the whole.

[45]Philo, *Flaccus* 74, 80; Josephus, *Jewish War,* VII, 412.

[46]Josephus, *Jewish War,* VII, 47.

[47]Cf. W.D. Davies, *The Gospel and the Land. Early Christianity and Jewish Territorial Doctrine* (Berkeley: University of California, 1974), 3-158.

3

Prominent People in House Churches

We have seen two broad contexts for understanding Paul's house churches, his own broad view of church and the Hellenistic world of those churches. With this background we can now focus on the details Paul gives about his churches and especially about the prominent personalities likely to be heads of such churches. We will survey the three localities about which Paul gives us the most information, Corinth, Rome, and the region of Colossae.

Corinth

The city of Corinth which Paul knew was the Roman city built over the ruins of the Greek city destroyed during the wars of Roman expansion. Situated on the narrow isthmus connecting the Peloponnesus with the rest of Greece, this Roman city prospered by its commerce, its banking, bronze artisanry, and of course government bureaucracy. A city where two-thirds of its estimated population of 600,000 were slaves, Corinth also displayed a highly vertical social structure. The rich were very rich and the poor often destitute. It was the province capital of Achaia, the lower half of Greece.

Paul's correspondence with the Corinthian church shows us a very diverse group, a group of very poor Christians, perhaps some very wealthy, and a substantial group of middle-class, probably well-off artisans and tradespeople. Understanding the extent of the wealth of the Corinthian Christians will shed some light on their House churches.

Paul in fact appeals to the material "abundance" (*perisseuma*) of the Corinthians to motivate them in his collection for the Jerusalem church (2 Cor 8:14). Since this abundance appears only in contrast to the lack of the Jerusalem church, it is difficult to evaluate the realism of Paul's remarks.

More telling are Paul's instructions concerning the manner in which to collect the money, namely, to put aside some money each week for the Jerusalem collection (1 Cor 16:1-4). Such an exercise would seem unnecessary for an aristocracy commanding capital and impossible for the destitute poor. Rather it would be a middle class with regular earnings that would find an "installment method" a practical way of accumulating a sizable collection for Paul.

In the same line, some Corinthians appear offended that Paul would not accept their monetary support and seem to have supported Paul's opponents (1 Cor 9:12-15; 2 Cor 11:7-12; 12:13). This attitude again sounds like a group which wants to display its resources and acquire the power that comes from patronage.

The practice of going to court in law suits is more difficult to interpret (1 Cor 6:1-11). Papyri of the time describe some small traders and village farmers going to court to complain about neighbors. However this practice is typical of those with property to protect, with a fair grasp of legal matters, with enough power to be confident of winning a suit, and with the ability to pay for a good attorney.

In this context, then, of a diverse church with a comfortable middle class, we can look at the prominent people of Corinth, who as property owners would be likely heads of house churches. Besides Paul's own writings to or about the Corinthians, the Lucan descriptions of Paul's work in Corinth (Acts 18) seem to provide reliable information.[1]

---

[1]Cf. G. Bornkamm, *Paul*, trans.D.M.G. Stalker (New York: Herder & Herder, 1969), p. 68, who, although extremely skeptical of the historical value of Acts for the life of Paul, writes, "The account in Acts furnishes reliable, detailed information about which there is no dispute (18:1-17)."; cf. also Malherbe, *Social Aspects*, p. 73, n. 27.

PRISCA AND AQUILA

Paul probably began his missionary work in Corinth around AD 52. In Acts 18 Luke describes the traditions and stories stemming from Paul's first visit, relating how Paul first met and took up lodging with Aquila and his wife Priscilla (whom Paul refers to as Prisca), a Jewish couple "recently" driven from Rome by the edict of Claudius (18:1-4). This emperor, according to Suetonius, expelled a number of Jews causing disturbances over a fellow called "Chrestos."[2] Most likely the disturbances involved Christian and non-Christian Jews in their fights about Christ.

Since Paul refers to Stephanas and his household, not Aquila and Prisca, as "the first fruits of Achaia," we probably must suppose that the Roman-Jewish couple were already Christian by the time Paul met them. Given the circumstances of their departure from Rome, an expulsion from troubles caused by Christians, their readiness to host Paul would be difficult to understand were they not already Christian. Later that pair will be responsible for house churches in Ephesus (1 Cor 16:19) and Rome (Rom 16:3).After the departure of Paul, their house is described as a place of Christian catechesis, at least for Apollos (Acts 18:26). It does not, therefore, sound risky to suppose that their house was functioning as a Christian house church by the time Paul met them. Luke's silence on the faith of Aquila and Priscilla would arise from his interest in presenting Paul as the founder of the faith in Corinth.

Dating the edict of Claudius, and hence the arrival of Aquila and Prisca at Corinth, is now a matter of controversy among scholars. Not long ago most investigators following the early Christian writer, Paulos Orosius (c. AD 417), dated Claudius' edict of expulsion to AD 49.[3] Other scholars today, looking to Dio Cassius, the second century writer,[4] see AD 41 as the date

---

[2] *Vita Claudii,* 25.

[3] *Historiae adversus Paganos,* 7,6,15f.

[4] *Roman History,* LX,6,6.

of the edict. The earlier we place this expulsion, the more time we can accord to the activity of Aquila and Prisca and their church in Corinth before Paul arrives as "founder."

Originally from the province of Pontus (along the coast of the Black Sea), Aquila appears as a tent maker or perhaps a leather worker (Acts 18:3). Hence Paul can use this household not only as a lodging, but also as a place to work. We can imagine a *collegia* or trade guild of tent makers in Corinth, to which Aquila belonged. Such a group would have afforded Paul further contacts in Corinth as well as some ideas for a *koinonia* of Christians beyond the individual household.

We know little about Prisca, but curious is the strong tendency to name her before her husband (Acts 18:18.19.26; Rom 16:3; 2 Tim 4:19; cf. opposite order in Acts 18:2; 1 Cor 16:19). This order may indicate a higher social status of Prisca over her husband. Aquila may have married the daughter of a wealthy and well-seen family. The ease with which this couple obtains property and establishes house churches on a tent maker's salary would otherwise be difficult to understand.

TITIUS JUSTICE

Luke describes Paul moving from the house of Priscilla and Aquila to that of Titius Justice, a "God-fearer" or Gentile co-worshiper with the Jews (Acts 18:7). The motive for the move is given as the location of Titius' house, namely, "next door to the synagogue." We probably should see Paul moving downtown from the suburban villa of Priscilla and Aquila. In this way Paul could have more contact with the Jewish community in the city.

Literary evidence abounds of a Jewish community in Corinth at the time of Paul.[5] No archeological evidence of this community, however, has been found, apart from a synagogue inscription which dates from a later time.

---

[5]Philo, *On the Embassy to Gaius*, 281; Justin, *Dialogue with Tryphon*, 1,3.

Titius appears as a good possible leader for the Christian community at Corinth. He owns a house big enough to host Paul. He also is obviously a man who had the courage and inner resources to break from paganism. As "the host of the Apostle," Titius would be distinguished in the community. He would be remembered some thirty years later when Luke was gathering the traditions of the church.

CRISPUS

Luke goes on to describe another major success for Paul in Corinth, the conversion of Crispus, the *archisynagōgos* of the Jewish community, along with his whole household (Acts 18:8). In his letter to the Corinthians, Paul speaks of Crispus as one of the few in Corinth that he personally baptized (1 Cor 1:14). Crispus' title shows up frequently in ancient inscriptions and generally designates the person who built the synagogue or who financed its regular maintenance out of his personal resources. In all probability, therefore, Crispus was a wealthy man.

Luke speaks of four household conversions, that of Cornelius "with all his house" in Caesarea (Acts 10:2), that of Lydia "and her house" in Philippi (Acts 16:15), that of Paul's jailer "with all in his house" also in Philippi (Acts 16:33), and Crispus "with his whole house" here in Corinth (Acts 18:8). All these households appear to be headed by people of some social status, a centurion, a business woman in a luxury item, a civil servant, and the *archisynagōgos*. Their conversions all occur during the initial stages of Paul's mission in these cities. If the households are remembered in the traditions of these cities, then we must see these households—not just the original head who converted—as having lasting significance for the Christian community of the later decades. In all likelihood, these households became prominent house churches in the development of the local church of these cities.

STEPHANAS

Stephanas and his household appear only in Paul's letter to the Corinthians. One of the few personally baptized by Paul (1 Cor 1:16), Stephanas and his household are singled out as "the first fruits" of Achaia, that is, the firt baptized or converted through Paul's efforts. Paul urges the Corinthians to recognize that Stephanas and his household "have established themselves (*etaxan heautous*) in the service (*diakonian*) of the saints" (16:15). The Corinthians in turn should "be subject" (*hypotassèsthe*) to such a household and to all who work with them (16:16). Paul in Ephesus is happy to see Stephanas who has traveled there with two associates (members of his household? slaves?), Fortunatus and Achaicus (16:17).

The verb Paul uses to describe the dedication of this household, *tassō*, emphasizes the established nature of their *diakonia*. Paul uses the verb elsewhere to describe being established in an office or power (Rom 13:1; cf. also Matt 8:9; Lk 7:8). The term can also have the more general meaning of "to determine, to appoint, to order," the meaning that fits the context in 1 Cor 16:15. Whatever the precise meaning, the expression here describes a dedicated activity, one characterizing the household as such, and one more stable or permanent than the usual sharing of gifts. Using a form of the same verb, Paul goes on to urge an ordered cooperation under this established service.

His property and his travels suggest Stephanas was a man of means. Such status coupled with the distinguished activity of the household points to a probable house church under him. We cannot be sure of the precise function of Stephanas, but we easily imagine him gathering his household with others into Christian assembly.

GAIUS

In his letter to the Romans, written from a suburb of Corinth, Paul sends regards and greetings from two more apparently prominent persons in the local church, Gaius and Erastus.

Paul describes Gaius as "my host (*xenos*) and that of the whole church" (*holēs tēs ekklēsias*, Rom 16:23). Gaius was the third person baptized by Paul (1 Cor 1:14).

While some commentators today see Gaius' role as providing only lodgings, not a place for assembly, early patristic exegesis saw in Gaius the owner of the house where the whole Corinthian community met. "The whole church" in 1 Cor 14:23 refers to a plenary assembly of Christians in the city, a type of meeting that appears also in 1 Cor 11:20 and 1 Thess 5:27. It is difficult to imagine how Gaius could provide lodgings "for the whole church," unless we read this expression as "the universal church," represented by the missionaries coming from all over and passing through Gaius' house. Such a reading, however, does not accord with Pauline usage of the key expression, "the whole church." More likely we should see Paul praising Gaius for allowing all the Corinthian Christians to gather in his dining room and atrium.

Gaius apparently had a very large dining room. Acts preserves a memory of "many" believers in Corinth (Acts 18:10). We cannot be sure of the accuracy of that memory, but if we add together just the members of the Christian households we have seen already we come up with a significant number. We probably have to think of the whole church of Corinth as including no less than thirty people. No poor person's house could accommodate such a number.

ERASTUS

Erastus is "the city treasurer" (*ho oikonomos tēs poleōs*) for the city of Corinth. Such an office was held by one of two types of persons: slaves employed in public accounting and finance, and prominent and wealthy people who functioned as important leaders in city government. These wealthy *oikonomoi* normally held the rank of *quaestor* and after their short term of office moved on to *aedil*. Paul does not usually refer to the social status of persons in the church. The only exception is Erastus, and Paul is probably not mentioning this office to publicize his dependent status. Furthermore we have later stories of independent travel by Erastus (Acts 19:22; 2 Tim 4:20). More likely than not, Erastus was another very wealthy person recruited by Paul and certainly another potential house church head.

An interesting inscription was found in Corinth mentioning a certain Erastus, who "laid the pavement out of his own money in order to obtain the rank of aedil."[6] The action describes the type of beneficence expected of aristocracy. Although the coincidence involved in the identification of this Erastus with the co-worker of Paul would be extraordinary, some scholars accept the possibility of this identification.

PHOEBE

In the letter to the Romans, Paul writes a line of recommendation for Phoebe, who is coming to Rome—presumably carrying the letter—and who obviously needs hospitality (Rom 16:1-2). Paul describes Phoebe as "our sister who is deacon (*diakonos*) of the church in Cenchreae" (Rom 16:1). Paul tells the Romans to receive her hospitably and to take care of all her necessities, "for she has been a *prostatis* to many and to me" (16:2).

The word *prostatis* is found in Greek literature to mean a "patroness," or "protectress." The masculine form *prostatēs* had a technical meaning in associated inscriptions as an executive or presiding officer. Paul uses a verbal form of this word with this meaning in 1 Thess 5:12. On the other hand, where Roman influence was strong, as was true for Corinth, *prostatēs* often translates the Latin word *patronus,* patron.

Since Paul never otherwise speaks of anyone presiding over him, we most probably should understand Phoebe's role as "patroness." Paul has in mind something more than general assistance on the part of Phoebe. He refers to her function as a motive to accord her generous hospitality. The term *prostatis*

6Text in J.H. Kent, *The Inscriptions 1926-1950. Corinth: Result of Excavations,* vol. 8, pt. 3 (Princeton: Princeton University, 1966), nr. 232.

apparently designates Phoebe as a wealthy patron of Paul, someone who has put her property at the service of Paul and of many others. She looks very much like the host of the community of Cenchreae, a church with its own identity but one connected in some way with the larger community of nearby Corinth.

Phoebe's name is taken from mythology. Such names were commonly given to slaves. Phoebe may be a freed woman. Her ability to make the long journey to Rome—with enough help to transport the hefty bundle of Paul's letter—shows an economic status consistent with our picture of her as a patron of the church.

Rome

Chapter 16 of Paul's letter to the Romans is our main source of knowledge about possible house churches in that city. Our analysis of this chapter, however, begins with a difficult question. Did Paul really write this chapter to the Romans?

The principal difficulty with seeing this chapter as part of the original letter to the Romans consists of some manuscript differences. One of the oldest papyrus manuscripts, p.[46] dating from c. AD 200, completely lacks Rom 16:1-23. Other manuscripts show strange shifts in the placement of the concluding doxology of Rom 16:25-27, occurring also after Rom 15:33 or after 14:23, or both after 14:23 and in its present location. These variants all suggest the existence of manuscripts that did not include the long list of greetings we presently find at the end of the letter.

Coupled with the unusually long list of names of people greeted in a city never visited by Paul, including some names connected with Ephesus like Prisca and Aquila (16:3-4) and Epaenetus (16:5), this manuscript evidence can argue for seeing chapter 16 either as a separate letter (of greetings?) or part of a letter (an Ephesian version of Romans?) sent to Ephesus.

More recent studies, however, are showing a growing acceptance of Romans 16 as part of the original letter.[7] The manuscript variations can be explained by attempts to "catholicize" the letter, that is, eliminate details that gear the instructions for a particular church. The long list of names is understandable in the light of Paul's purpose for writing, namely, to introduce himself to the Roman Christians and to be accepted by them.

As describing the Christians of Rome known to Paul, Rom 16:3-16 presents us with at least three groups of Christians and maybe more. Paul first sends greetings to Prisca and Aquila and their house church (16:3-5). Of all the people mentioned in these greetings, this couple receive the highest praise. They apparently risked their lives during Paul's imprisonment in Ephesus. Paul goes out of his way to recommend this Jewish pair to the predominantly Gentile Christian community in Rome. "To them go not only my thanks but those of all the churches of the Gentiles" (16:4). Paul may be suspecting some difficulty of this couple's being accepted in Rome after their return from banishment.

A list of fourteen individuals and groups from two different households then follow in verses 5b-13. Several of these appear as particularly dear to Paul. Several are called "beloved" or "beloved in the Lord": Ampliatos, who bears a common slave name (16:8); Stachus (16:9); and Persis, who also bears a common female slave name (16:12). Paul feels dear enough to Rufus and his mother to be a member of this family (16:13). Others are described as associated with Paul in some way: Andronicus and Junia, Paul's co-prisoners (16:7); Urbanus ("Man from the City"), a co-worker (16:9). To this list we should probably add Epaenetus ("Highly Praised"), the first fruit of Asia (16:5). Like Prisca and Aquila, these people have all obviously spent some time with Paul. Perhaps like Prisca and Aquila, and probably Epaenetus, these people worked with Paul in Ephesus, where some were also imprisoned with him. If indeed these persons worked together in Ephesus, they

[7]Cf. Harry Y. Gamble, *The Textual History of the Letter to the Romans* (Ph.D. Dissertation; Yale University, 1971).

probably moved to Rome together, where Prisca and Aquila could host their number in their house church.

Another salient point in the list is the number of names which are either typically Jewish or at least attested as naming a Jewish person: Mary; Andronicus and Junia; Apelles, greeted as "proven in Christ" (16:10); Herodion, specifically described as of the same race as Paul (16:11), and Tryphaena, named with Tryphosa, thought to be her sister (16:12). As Jews these Christians would presumably have been under the same ban as Prisca and Aquila and hence also recent arrivals. As Jewish Christians they would have another bond to Prisca and Aquila-all of which again suggests membership in Prisca and Aquila's house church.

Among these individuals several, particularly the women, stand out as prominent Christians. Paul describes four women, Mary, Tryphaena, Tryphosa, and Persis, as persons who have labored much or labored in Christ. Paul describes this activity with the verb, *kopiaō,* which he uses several times to describe his own intense apostolic work (1 Cor 15:10; Gal 4:11; Phil 2:16; Col 1:29; cf. also 1 Cor 16:16).

Paul describes Andronicus and Junia as "outstanding among the apostles" (16:7). Junia's name has suffered much in a transmission which tended to turn her into a man, probably because she is called an apostle. The accusative form in which her name occurs in this verse, *Iounian,* could conceivably be the accusative form of something like *Iounias,* a man's name in form but which is hardly ever found naming a man. On the contrary, the name *Iounia,* which also has the accusative *Iounian,* is a common name for a woman. In the middle ages, when accents began to be used in writing, the common accusative spelling could be distinguished for man or woman by accenting the last syllable or second to the last syllable respectively. By that time Junia had become a man. There was no doubt, however, in the mind of the Greek-speaking theologian and church leader of the 4th century, John Chrysostom, who wrote, "How great is the *philosophia* of this woman that she is held to be worthy of the name of apostle."[8]

---

[8]*Comment. in Epistulam ad Romanos, Homilia.* 31, 2 (PG 60/669f).

Along with the individuals of verses 5b-13 are two groups named from households: "those of [the household of] Aristobulus" (16:10) and "those of [the household of] Narcissus who are in the Lord" (16:11). The expression Paul uses for these two groups is the same in form as the one he uses for the imperial slaves and freedmen who were employed as civil servants throughout the empire, "those of [the house of] Caesar" (Phil 4:22). Paul does not use this expression for a house church.

Hence, the groups named in the greetings of Romans 16 appear to be the Christian slaves and free servants from prominent Roman households. Aristobulus may be the famous brother or the nephew of Herod Agrippa I. We have no idea who Narcissus could be, but Paul's effort to specify the Christian members of Narcissus' household suggests he himself was not Christian. Both groups thus are probably the Christian slaves and servants of non-Christian households. To gather as church these persons would have to associate with a Christian household, again perhaps that of Prisca and Aquila—whose house is looking larger and larger as we continue our speculations.

This supposition of the Christians of 16:5b-13 all forming a single house church entails some interesting consequences. Presumably Aquila, (with his wife, Prisca?) would be the head of the house church. Membership would include such important persons as apostles, who have a special priority over all other offices (1 Cor 12:28). Such a group would be predominately Jewish Christian, suggesting that the division between Gentile and Jewish Christians found expression in distinct house churches. Finally, this group would extend far beyond the household of Prisca and Aquila and in fact include several other families. From Prisca and Aquila's house church, we get an idea of how open and inclusive the house church could be.

In verse 14, however, Paul greets another group: Asyncritus ("the Incomparable"); Phlegon, who bears a common slave name; Hermes, who bears a mythological name as did many slaves; Patrobas; Hermas, and "the brothers who are with them" (*tous syn autois adelphous*). Although no woman is mentioned, this group seems to form something like a house church.

Similarly in verse 15 Paul greets a group: Philologus, a common slave name, and Julia, clearly his wife; Nereus, another mythological name, and his sister (wife?); Olympas; and "all the holy ones who are with them" (*tous syn autois pantas hagious*). Again this group seems to form something like a house church, although again as for the preceding group, Paul does not use the term "church" to describe them. "Brothers" and "Holy ones" are expressions used by Paul for Christians whom he identifies as a "church" (1 Cor 1:2; cf. 1:10; 1 Thess 1:4; cf. 1:1; Phil 1:1; cf. 4:15). The omission might be simply linguistic.

Was there any local church of Rome like that of Corinth, Philippi, or Thessalonica? Paul does not greet the Roman Christians with this term. He never refers to them as a church, and he is silent about them ever "gathering in the same place." All this silence suggests that Paul did not see these Christians as a church.

The one indication to the contrary is Paul's instruction at the end of the letter, "Greet one another with a holy kiss" (16:16). Paul gives this instruction to the Corinthians (1 Cor 16:20; 2 Cor 13:12) and the Thessalonians (1 Thess 5:26), who clearly form a city-wide church. On the other hand 1 Peter, addressed to Christians throughout Pontus, Galatia, Cappadocia, Asia, and Bithynia (1:1) likewise ends with this instruction (5:14), suggesting that the instruction may be a literary formality.

Later documents show the development of a city-church in Rome. *I Clement,* dated in the range AD 75-110, describes itself in its salutations as coming from "the church of God sojourning in Rome." Around AD 155 Saint Justin describes the usual Christian gathering in Rome on "the day of the Sun." It is "a meeting in the same place (*epi to auto syneleusis*) of all those dwelling in the cities and fields."[9] In the record of his trial testimony dated some ten years later, Justin is described as saying,

---

[9] *1 Apology,* 67,3.

I have been staying above the baths of Myrtinus [?] for the whole time in which I resided in Rome for this second time. And I know of no other meeting place except the one there. If anyone wishes to come to me there, I would share with him the words of truth.[10]

The meeting place "above the baths" sounds very much like either an insula apartment or more likely a second floor *domus*. An apartment would not seem to be large enough to house a city-church. The insistence on the uniqueness of the location corresponds to Justin's own description of the Christians meeting together. His availability to anyone seeking instruction suggests that the place was Justin's normal residence.

This later evidence shows a tendency toward the city-wide church. Perhaps the Christians of Rome at the time of Paul had not cohered into a church. But apparently the dynamisms were in place in the house churches of Rome to bring about a city-wide church.

Asia

The Roman province of Asia embraced roughly the western quarter of today's Turkey. Paul's work there was centered in Ephesus, the capital of the province. He mentions that city as the place from which he wrote 1 Corinthians (1 Cor 16:8), from where also he sends regards from "the churches of Asia" (16:19). Luke records a tradition of Paul spending over two years in that city (Acts 19:10).

Colossae lay about 100 miles east of Ephesus, up the Lycus river valley. Not far away across the valley lay Laodicea, a much larger city, and Hierapolis, known for its sacred spas.

Paul speaks to the Christians of Colossae and Laodicea as to persons whom he had never visited, "you and those in Laodicea and all the others who have not seen my face in the

---

[10] *Passio sancti Justini et socii* 3.3.

flesh" (Col 2:1; cf. also 1:4). Paul apparently never stopped at these cities on his way to Ephesus. We can imagine, however, Paul sending his missionaries to places like Colossae to found churches under his supervision. In any case Epaphras, founder and a leader of the Christian community in Colossae, comes to Paul for help when problems get out of hand (Col 1:7).

The most important link of Philemon to the Lycus valley churches is his slave Onesimus. Speaking to the Colossians Paul names apparently the same Onesimus as "one of you" (4:9). Such a description would imply that Philemon, of whose household Onesimus was a member, was also a citizen of Colossae. Likewise Paul addresses apparently the same Archippus in the letter to the Colossians (4:17) as he greets in his letter to Philemon and whom he associates with Philemon and his house church (v. 2). These persons common to the letters suggest Philemon lived in Colossae. Yet Paul seems to presume a close friendship with Philemon, from whom he expects hospitality and through whose prayers he hopes to be pardoned (v. 22). It is difficult to see how this friendship could be possible if Philemon was one of the Colossians who had never met Paul.

The problem of Philemon's connection with Colossae does not completely go away if we consider Colossians to be Deutero-Pauline. We would still have to deal with a letter that tries to strengthen the fiction of Pauline authorship by alluding to traditions linking people like Onesimus and Archippus to Colossae.

Whatever their exact relationship with Paul may be, these cities along with Ephesus are mentioned by Paul as locations of house churches. We can identify at least three such house churches and perhaps more.

PRISCA AND AQUILA

In Ephesus Paul sends the Corinthians greetings from Prisca and Aquila and their house church. Before the mention of Prisca and Aquila, Paul sends greetings of all the churches of Asia. After mentioning them he sends the greetings of "all the brothers" (1 Cor 16:19). Acts records the tradition of Prisca and Aquila traveling with Paul from Corinth to Ephesus (AD 53?) and there establishing a house where Christian catechesis took place (Acts 18:18-19.26). Although the scope of the greetings at the end of Corinthians includes those from all of Asia, we should most likely locate the house church of Prisca and Aquila in Ephesus.

The very way Paul singles out this house church suggests the existence of other Christians in Ephesus. The greetings from "all the brothers" probably refer to the other Christians in Ephesus, besides those who meet in Prisca and Aquila's church.

Acts is silent about the Jewish Christian pair when it describes Paul's extended stay in that city (AD 55-57?). Perhaps Prisca and Aquila along with a number of other Jewish Christians had returned to Rome. AD 55 was the year of the death of Claudius and hence the end of his ban.

Acts gives us the example of Prisca and Aquila in Ephesus accepting the responsibility of instructing Apollos, a fellow Jewish Christian. The house church of this couple may in fact have been one geared for Jewish Christians. As we saw in our examination of the Roman communities, a large number of Jewish Christians appear with Prisca and Aquila in the list of greetings, many of whom have recently been with Paul. One, Epaenetus, is specifically connected with Asia. Some probability suggests these Christians now in Rome formed the bulk of the membership of Prisca and Aquila's house church in Ephesus. Together, after the lifting of Claudius' ban in AD 55, they would have returned to Rome.

PHILEMON

The next house church mentioned in an undisputed letter of Paul is that of Philemon. Despite the personal character of the letter, Paul addresses it not only to Philemon but Apphia, most probably his wife, Archippus, and Philemon's house church (vv. 1-2). We can presume that Archippus would be a member of this house church.

The broad scope of the greeting reflects Paul's sense of being an apostle. Whatever he does has a certain public character. He consistently associates people with himself as author—in this case Timothy—and he writes to congregations.

A curious but typical ambiguity appears in Philemon's relationship with Paul. The ambiguity involves the two most common ways an active person like Paul could enlist the participation of another. On the one hand Philemon appears as Paul's patron (*prostatēs*). He hosts Paul. As an apparently wealthy person, he in fact generously provides the material that Paul needs. As we saw private religious groups depended heavily on rich patrons especially to provide a place to meet. The patron was then singled out with extravagant honors and privileges.

On the other hand Philemon appears as Paul's partner (*koinōnos*). Paul expressly uses the term, "If you hold me then as a partner (*koinōnon*), receive Onesimus as you would me" (v. 17). In Greco-Roman law and society, the *koinōnos* or *socius* often provided the money for a business venture, could be held responsible for debts, and profited by success. Because the partner did not have the power that a patron had over the man in the field, Paul feels more comfortable with this relationship. Paul could come to Philemon's house as "the apostle," without having to deal with special protocol toward a patron.

COLOSSIAN HOUSE CHURCHES?

Any investigation of the relationship of Philemon's house church to the nearest local church runs into the problem of the location of this house church. If the location is Colossae then the distinction of the house church from the city-wide group is reflected in the distinction of the two letters. No church of the Colossians is mentioned in Philemon, nor, even more curiously, is Philemon mentioned in Colossians—while members of Philemon's house church are.

The problem is compounded by an emphasis on "universal church" in Colossians. "The holy ones at Colossae" are never called a church, which in this letter seems to be a more heavenly, cosmic reality. Nevertheless, we have church activities described:

> Let the word of Christ dwelling in you fully, teaching and admonishing one another in all wisdom, by psalms, hymns and spiritual songs, in charity singing in your hearts to God (3:16).

> Persevere in prayer. With it keep vigils in thanksgiving, praying together and for us (4:2).

Sandwiched between these instructions dealing with more or less cultic activities, Paul gives his "household code," providing special instructions to husbands, wives, children, fathers, slaves, and masters (3:18-4:1). The juxtaposition of the material suggests that home life was not far from church life.

NYMPHA

The house church mentioned in Colossians is not that of Philemon but that of Nympha, presumably in Laodicea. Paul asks the Colossians, "Greet the brothers in Laodicea and Nympha and her house church" (4:15). Nympha's house church seems to be grouped with the brothers at Laodicea. Another possibility would be to see Nympha's house church in the nearby city of Hierapolis. Paul mentions the existence of Christians in both Laodicea and Hierapolis (4:13). However, the context of 4:15, where Nympha is mentioned, deals with Laodicea. Furthermore, Paul continues in 4:16 to instruct the Colossians about exchanging letters with Laodicea.

In the transmission of the text, Nympha unfortunately suffered the same mistreatment as Junia; she was quickly made a man, most probably because a woman leader in the church would have been scandalous to later scribes. Like Junia in the accusative case without any accents (found only in later manuscripts), Nympha's name could be read as either masculine or feminine. As masculine, NYMPHAN would be the accusative form of Nymphas, an abbreviated form of Nymphodorus. As feminine, it would be the accusative form of Nympha, a Doric form for the Attic woman's name Nymphe. The ambiguity is resolved, however, with the personal pronoun that follows and connects the person to the house church. It is with this pronoun that the scribes took their stand.

Reading "her (*autēs*) church" is one of the oldest (4th century) and most carefully copied manuscripts of the bible, codex B, along with a number of much later manuscripts. This is the reading known to Origen and to the translators of some very early Syriac and Coptic versions.

Reading "his (*autou*) church" is the famous D ("Western") manuscript, a 6th century document noted for its frequent divergences from more reliable traditions, followed by some important manuscripts of the 9th century and 11th century. Stemming from Erasmus, doing the best he could with the limited number of manuscripts of his time to provide a critical edition of the Greek New Testament, the *Textus Receptus* tradition popularized this reading in many European translations, including the translation of the King James Bible.

A third reading attested very early is "their (*autōn*) church," which is most likely an attempt to involve "the brothers" at Laodicea in this house church.

The editors of the modern "Kurt Aland" critical edition of the Greek New Testament have decided for "her church." The decision is very reasonable, based not only on the reliability of the manuscripts but also on the probability of the change from one reading to the other. The later scribes would be more likely to change "her church" to "his church" for theological reasons. It is difficult to imagine why a scribe would have felt the need to change "his church" to "her church." The overall evidence seems compelling in favor of "her church," the more difficult reading and the best attested by manuscripts. With this conclusion we can place Nympha with Prisca and Lydia, as heads of house churches in the Pauline world of Christianity.

If we locate Nympha's church in Laodicea, we then have a house church within a local church. Paul refers to the Christians of Laodicea as an *ekklēsia* (4:16). We can only guess about the relationship between these "levels" of church. We have no hint of the leadership among "the brothers" of Laodicea. We do not know to what degree Nympha's church would gather with "the church of the Laodiceans." However, none of the problems addressed by the letter to the Colossians, which was to be read by the Laodiceans, deal with church disunity.

4

Positions of Leadership in the Church

In a rudimentary form, offices of leadership existed in the Pauline churches, not the ecclesiastical offices we are familiar with, but positions within the church with some degree of permanence and enough formalization to distinguish the persons with those functions, even to the degree of carrying a title. Some of these offices seem to stem from a broad sense of church, particularly one rooted in the primitive Jerusalem church. Others seem directly connected with the house church structure.

In 1 Corinthians and Romans Paul gives us three lists of leaders and functions. In other letters he makes brief mention of individual positions. The lists show considerable variation, indicating extensive freedom for spontaneous or charismatic forms of leadership. Paul shows, however, some consistency in mentioning roles and at least once insists on a ranking of some of those roles. Hence some degree of formalization of leadership and functions, some relative permanence appear in the Pauline churches.

The lists are as follows:

1 Cor 12:28-30	*1 Cor 12:8-10*	*Rom 12:6-8*
first apostles	word of wisdom	prophecy
second prophets	word of knowledge	*diakonia*
third teachers	faith	the teacher
then miracles	healing	the exhorter

then gifts of healing	worker of wonders	the sharer (*ho meta-didous*)
assistance	prophecy	the patron (*ho pro-istamenos*)
leadership	discerning spirits	the one showing mercy
kinds of tongues	kinds of tongues	
interpret (v. 30)	interpretation of tongues	

We will examine these lists in detail along with his mention of "bishops (*episkopoi*) and deacons (*diakonoi*)" at Philippi (Phil 1:1).

As we can see from the variety of the names, the purpose of Paul's listing is neither to be exhaustive nor to designate mutually exclusive roles and activities. Paul's point is rather to illustrate how all have some gift from God for the good of the gathering. Paul's explicit concern is to demonstrate the mutual dependence of all members of the church. These roles are gifts whose harmony and mutuality are rooted in the one God and the one Spirit responsible for them all.

In 1 Corinthians 12 Paul stresses the nature of gift to such an extent, we could conclude to a picture of a purely spontaneous community, one waiting for the Spirit to determine the roles:

> The one and the same Spirit produces all these [gifts], distributing by himself (*idia*) to each one as he wills (12:11).

Using this description of Paul, some have imagined a strict egalitarianism in at least the church of Corinth. Closer examination shows that the basis of the distribution was not that simple.

Taken together the lists seem to include three types of roles, one which appears mostly clearly as offices, "apostles, prophets, and teachers"; another which shows up least as an office, the miraculous functions in the community; and a third group of administrators who are somewhere between the other two in formality of role.

1. Apostles, Prophets, and Teachers

The "apostles," "prophets," and "teachers" form one group distinguished in the lists. They appear with a high degree of formality.

The role of "apostle" is rooted in the traditions of "the twelve" special disciples of Jesus. As sent by Jesus, these apostles represented Jesus, much like the Jewish *shaliach,* sent out to collect the temple tax, represented the top authorities. While the Synoptics limit the apostles to "the Twelve," Paul has a wider view, in which he includes, not only "the apostles before him" in Jerusalem (Gal 1:17), but also himself (Rom 1:1, 1 Cor 1:1, etc.), his associates Silvanus and Timothy (1 Thess 2:6), Andronicus and Junia (Rom 16:7), the "super-apostles" causing trouble in Corinth (2 Cor 11:5), and perhaps "the apostles of the churches" in 2 Cor 8:11. On the other hand as applied to Epaphroditus, "ambassador" of the Philippians (Phil 2:25), the term "apostle" does not seem to be an office but a general description.

Sometime after the death of Paul, the letter to the Ephesians describes the apostles as constituting with the prophets "the foundation" of the house of God (2:20) and as the primary recipients of God's new revelation (3:5). We have here a widely recognized office, the importance and authority of which was unsurpassed in the church.

While the original apostles of Jesus seem to have remained in Jerusalem forming something like a governing council, travel seems to be part of the other apostles' job description. They do not seem to be officials so much within the local churches, as rather visitors representing a larger view of the church, founding local churches by their preaching of the Gospel.

In the Pauline churches, the clearest example of an apostle in action is Paul himself. Although he rarely commands, Paul is conscious of the authority (*exousia*) given him by the Lord to build up (2 Cor 10:8; 13:10). At moments of crisis he intervenes with great vigor in the life of the community, expecting obedience (2 Cor 2:9; Phil 2:12; Phlm 21).

Paul's apostolic "work" (*ergon*), however, is not a part of the normal life of the local *ekklēsia*. Most of the time he is away from any given local church, whose self-sufficiency he frequently recognizes (1 Thess 4:8; 1 Cor 2:15-16; Rom 8:9-17; 15:14). His interventions by way of letters and emissaries are geared toward special problems and questions.

"Prophets and teachers" appear in a wide range of early Christian literature. In the Lucan description of the church of Antioch they together form an important group of leaders (Acts 13:1). The Gospel of Matthew, which probably also reflects the church of Antioch, speaks of prophecy as a common phenomenon of the church and urges hospitality toward apparently itinerant prophets (Matt 10:40-41; cf. 7:22). 1 Thess 5:19-20 appears to be Paul's defense of prophecy in the church of the Thessalonians. Ephesians as we have seen links prophets with apostles as the foundation of the church (2:20) and the primary recipients of God's new revelation (3:5). The Book of Revelation and the Didache likewise presuppose the existence of Christian prophets in the churches of the late first century.

The actual functioning of the prophet can be seen from two perspectives. Paul describes the work of the prophets in terms of "building up the church" (1 Cor 14:4), especially by words of "encouragement and comfort" (14:3) along with "exposing," "judging," and "laying bare" the hearts of unbelievers (14:24-25). If, however, as is most probable, Christian prophecy arose out of Jewish apocalyptic, the function of the prophet in the church was in fact more likely in the line of revealing divine secrets, often in the form of dreams, visions, and oracles.[1] Paul seems to refer to this apocalyptic side of prophecy, when he compares it unfavorably with the gift of love, "If I had prophecy and I knew all the mysteries and all knowledge . . . " (1 Cor 13:2). Likewise the prophecy for which Paul apparently urges testing sounds like an apocalyptic brand (1 Thess 5:20-21). His descriptions of the more "edifying" functions of

---

[1]Cf. G. Dautzenberg, *Urchristliche Prophetie. Ihre Erforschung, ihre Vorausetzungen im Judentum und ihre Struktur im ersten Korintherbrief* (Stuttgart: Kohlhammer, 1975).

prophecy might be his typical way of trying to deemphasize the apocalyptic or miraculous side without squelching the function as such.

It is hard to estimate the amount of travel expected of a prophet. Late in the 1st century, the itinerant prophet seems to be the norm. The *Didache* gives us a clear description of such a propertyless person (13:1). On the other hand, the function of the prophet in the Pauline church and especially Paul's rules regarding the exercise of prophecy (1 Cor 11:4-5; 14:1-40) suggest a more established person. However, the admonition in Matthew to offer prophets hospitality testifies to the existence of traveling prophets (Matt 10:40-41). Luke gives us the picture of the Christian prophet, Agabos, who is frequently on the move (Acts 11:27-28; 21:10). Likewise when Luke designates Paul and Barnabas as "prophets and teachers" on the eve of their missionary journey, he suggests that travel may have been an expected part of these offices.

Teachers (*didaskaloi*) probably functioned in the church much like those Jews who bore the same name—giving instructions, delivering ethical exhortations, receiving, preserving, transmitting the tradition, interpreting Scripture. As used in Christian circles, the title has its roots in the Hebrew or Aramaic identification of Jesus as "rabbi" or *didaskalos,* the Greek translation of the Hebrew (Jn 1:38). The Christian teacher was probably responsible for the traditions about Jesus, the narratives of his actions, the collections of his sayings, as well as the kerygmatic formulas used in the church.

The figure of Apollos, the Jewish Christian versed in Scripture and man of eloquence who spoke and taught about Jesus, as well as the figures of Prisca and Aquila, who completed the religious instruction of Apollos, present us with typical Christian *didaskaloi* (Acts 18:24-28).

Paul refers to the same office in his mention of *ho katēchōn,* with whom the *katēchoumenos* should share his goods (Gal 6:6). The "teacher" is thus in need of support. By insisting on the need of the community to support the "teacher," Paul may be indicating either 1) that some of the residents of a local church had dedicated themselves more or less full-time to religious teaching and therefore needed community support or 2) that some of these teachers like Paul traveled from city to city.

Earlier Paul elaborated on the right of apostles like himself to be supported by their work ("You shall not muzzle the ox", 1 Cor 9:3-14). Although Paul chose not to exercise this right and to support himself by his tentmaking, the need for support arises particularly for ministers who like Paul traveled from one community to another. Paul was fortunate in being able to join in the work of Prisca and Aquila in Corinth. Such ease of immediate employment would not be something an itinerant minister could always count on. Those who followed the life style of Jesus, giving up home and property for the sake of the gospel, needed to count on the "hundred-fold" brothers, sisters, and homes for material support.

The figure of Apollos gives us a clear example of the itinerant teacher (cf. Acts 18:24-28; 1 Cor 16:12; Tit 3:12). On the other hand, the resident teachers, Prisca and Aquila, exemplify persons with self-supporting employment (Acts 18:3).

What is important for our study is the apparent Jewish and even Palestinian roots for all three religious offices, apostle, prophet, and teacher. Of all the functions listed by Paul, these three are the most formalized. Whereas the other functions are listed by verbs ("working miracles," "distinguishing spirits") or by actions ("healing," assistance"), "apostle," "prophet," and "teacher" clearly name offices. They are the only ones explicitly given in an order. These three are the offices responsible for founding churches, teaching and guiding the members, transmitting divine revelations, expounding Scripture, and thus formulating God's will in the concrete circumstances of daily life.

All three have roots in the earliest strata of Christianity, either in the figure of Jesus himself or that of his first disciples. All three appear in churches wider than the Pauline circle. The triad probably originated in Palestinian or Antiochan Christianity, and forms a legacy of Jewish Christianity. These three offices are part of one of the earliest church "structures" to develop, one which Paul inherited and incorporated into his work.

Given the formal and essential character of these offices, it seems unlikely that any Christian claiming the gift could function as an apostle, prophet or teacher. Much more likely the three titles named special groups of people, recognized in some way by the community, who could be depended on for reliable service in these roles. Thus when Paul incorporates "apostle," "prophet," and "teacher" into the list of the free gifts of the Spirit, he is pointing out not so much that anyone can be an apostle, prophet, or teacher, as rather that the gifts of being an apostle, prophet or teacher are three of many more gifts of the Spirit. One does not have to be one of these three to be gifted of the Spirit and an essential member of the body.

In the same line, it would seem unlikely that we would find these offices in every house church. The "apostle" clearly seems to be an office rooted in the interrelationship of churches and seems to be present only occasionally even in the local churches. The "prophets" like "teachers" probably came in two models, the itinerants and the residents. The itinerant prophets and teachers, like the apostles, linked the city-churches together. Even the prophets and teachers in residence seemed to function far more on the level of the local church than on that of the private house church.

2. Miracles

The other roles in the lists of gifts show a great deal more variety in wording. The list of 1 Cor 12:28-30 includes other types of functions. One group includes spectacular, even miraculous, functioning in the church. After apostles, prophets, and teachers, Paul mentions "miracles" and "gifts of healing" (12:28). These have their direct counterparts in the early list: "healing," "worker of wonders," and most probably "faith" (12:9-10). At the end of both lists is a second group, "kinds of tongues" and "interpretation of tongues" (12:10.30).

Paul does not mention such spectacular roles in other churches. These are the special gifts in which the Corinthians seemed to have great interest. Their prominence in 1 Corinthians 12 basically prepares for the discussion of the superiority of prophecy over tongues (ch. 14) and the supremacy of charity over all forms of miracles (ch. 13).

Miracles and tongues, along with their related gifts, were clearly the most "charismatic" of the gifts, that is, seen as entirely and exclusively dependent on an action of the Spirit, as manifestations of the Spirit's freedom. These powers were relatively independent of human administration. The emphasis on such gifts in the Corinthian church would suggest an overall tone in the church favoring the freedom of the Spirit over human management.

3. *Administrators and Leaders*

Paul, however, squeezes into the list a passing mention of "assistances" (*antilēmspeis*) and "leadership" (*kybernēseis*, 1 Cor 12:28). Neither term comes up for discussion nor is even repeated in the following echo of the list (12:29-30). Their position here between miracles and tongues may be a subtle attempt by Paul to tone down the spectacular character of the gifts or at least to show how the Spirit brings along his own forms of administration according to which a certain orderliness can be imposed on the more charismatic functions.

Like the preceding "miracles" and "healing," the two terms "assistances" and "leadership" look like two aspects of the same role. In this case the leading function derives from the assistance given.

This is the only time the two terms, *antilēmspeis* and *kybernēseis*, appear in the New Testament. They, therefore, show no indication of having an officially stabilized meaning as technical terms. Nothing here indicates that Paul inherited these categories from Judeo-Christianity or any other earlier group.

In the list of Rom 12:6-8 we see similar functions. There Paul mentions "the sharer" (*ho metadidous*), "the patron" (*ho proistamenos*), and "the almsgiver" (*ho eleōn*). These three names, all participles, last in the list, fall somewhat together.

Paul joined the previous names in the list with the conjunction "whether ... whether...." He lists these last names without conjunction (asyndetically).

Paul uses the verb *metadidōmi* frequently to refer to "sharing" the gospel or some spiritual gift (1 Thess 2:8; Rom 1:11).The word is used for distributing material things (Lk 3:11) and at times becomes almost a technical term for almsgiving (Rom 12:8; Eph 4:28; *Hermas,* visions, III, 9, 2.4). Translating the participle, *ho metadidous,* as "the sharer" is an attempt to capture the breadth of this word.

The verb *eleeō* in the New Testament generally means "to be merciful and forgiving," an action describing God's merciful love and the duty of all Christians. The term can also mean "to do acts of mercy" in the sense of charitable giving.[2] The related noun *eleēmosynē,* specifically means a charitable donation. Since Paul in this list is singling out a specific function, the term *ho eleōn* should be translated as "the almsgiver."

In content "the sharer" and "the almsgiver" appear as parallel synonyms, all referring to practical and material support on the part of a person of some wealth. Included between these two, *ho proistamenos,* should, therefore, likewise be read as more or less synonymous with the others.

The verb *proistēmi,* for which *proistamenos* is the participle, can have a general sense of "to care for" or "to give aid." It can also have the more specific sense of "to be at the head of," "to rule or direct," particularly as one directs or manages one's household (cf. 1 Tim 3:4-5). As previously mentioned, the noun form of this verb *prostatēs* (fem. *prostatis*) often refers to a "patron," especially in Roman areas of the empire, where the word was translated as *patronus.* Translating *proistamenos* as "patron" fits the synonymous parallelism of the three names at the end of the list. The adverbial phrase here modifying this function, *en spoudē,* confirms this translation. In Gal 2:10 *spoudasa* describes Paul's efforts for the poor.

Most probably, then, the three words "the sharer," "the

---

[2]Cf. *Didache,* 2:7.

patron," and "the almsgiver" refer to the same role, the person of wealth in the community, the property owner, who now sees this wealth as a gift of God to be managed well for the benefit of God's people. We have here the manager or administrator in the church.

This list of Rom 12 contains also the work of *diakonia,* slipped in between "prophecy" and "teacher." In the literature of the time, this term is never associated with any particular dignity or position. It is used for "service" (1 Macc 11:58; Est 6:3). In Philo and Josephus, *diakonia* refers to waiting at tables.[3] Paul uses this Greek term to describe his own work in the broadest terms (Rom 11:13; 2 Cor 4:1; 5:18; 6:3; 11:8), as well as the work of Stephanas and his household (1 Cor 16:15) and Archippus (Col 4:17). Synonymous with *charismata* and *energēmata, diakonia* can refer to all the gifts of the Spirit (1 Cor 12:5).

Only when used for the work of collecting or providing money (Rom 15:31; 2 Cor 8:4; 9:1.12.13), does the term take on a specific sense. In fact, referring to the collection of money for the poor of Jerusalem, Paul seems to give the term an almost technical sense,

> Struggle with me in prayer ... in order that I be rescued from the unbelievers in Judea and that my *diakonia* for Jerusalem become accepted by the holy ones (Rom 15:30-31).

If Paul intends the word as used in this list of church functions to have a specific meaning, somehow distinguishable from the other roles in the list, he may well mean the term to refer to some administration of money.

If we turn to the occasional mention of leadership in the church outside of these lists, we find a variety of terms all more or less referring to the same type of function, that of the

---

[3]Philo, *On the Contemplative Life,* 70; Josephus, *Jewish Antiquities,* II,65; XI,163.166.

administrator who provides material support for the community and as a result functions as administrator and leader.

In the final exhortations of 1 Thessalonians, the patron or *proistamenos* appears again. Paul tells his readers to recognize "those laboring among you." The verb (*kopiaō*) is the same Paul uses to refer to his own missionary enterprises (1 Cor 15:10; Gal 4:11; Phil 2:16; Col 1:29). Without distinguishing them as separate groups (both under one article), Paul then refers to "your patrons (*proistamenoi*) and admonishers (*nouthetountes*) in the Lord" (1 Thess 5:12).The activity of these people deals with care concerned with concrete needs as well as some form of verbal discipline in moral matters. Paul acknowledges their work without reserve and requests the church to recognize them and hold them in high esteem.

Concluding 1 Corinthians Paul asks his readers to submit themselves to Stephanas, his household, and all who labor (*synergounti kai kopiōnti*) with them (1 Cor 16:15-16). The activity for which Stephanas is recognized is described as a *diakonia* of the holy ones. This name corresponds to the second in the list of Rom 12:6-8, mentioned after prophecy and before teacher. Nothing is said here about a special appointment, rather it would appear that Stephanas and his household attain this priority in the Corinthian church on their own initiative. They responded first (as "first fruits") to Paul's missionary work.

Greeting the Philippians, Paul names "bishops and deacons" (*episkopoi kai diakonoi*) who are addressed with "all the holy ones" in Philippi (Phil 1:1). These titles will function prominently in the later church to designate in a technical way very specific offices. However, we must be careful not to read into the text of Philippians this technical significance.

The term *diakonos,* like its abstract relative *diakonia,* shows up outside the New Testament mostly for persons more or less directly involved in waiting on tables.[4] Paul uses the term

---

[4]For references cf. F. Poland, *Geschichte des griechischen Vereinswesens* (Preisschriften ... der Fuerstlich Jablonowskischen Gesellschaft, 38; Leipzig: 1909) 391-93.

diakonos in a variety of contexts, best translated by the general English word, "minister." The civil ruler is God's "minister" (Rom 1:4). Paul is a "minister of the new covenant" (2 Cor 3:6), "of God" (6:4), "of the gospel" (Col 1:23), and "of the church" (1:25). He shares the title with Phoebe (Rom 16:1), Apollos (1 Cor 3:5), Epaphras (Col 1:7), Tychicus (4:7), and Timothy (1 Thess 3:2). Outside of Philippi, the term seems to have even less specificity than the term *diakonia*.

The term *episkopos* had a more precise meaning in contemporary Greek. It is first used with the general sense of "overseer," functioning as "watcher," "protector," or "patron," whose activity was a gracious overseeing and care of the one protected.[5] In the later voluntary associations, the *episkopoi* were men and women in relatively minor offices, overseeing various activities or other people. When it can be distinguished, their work usually involved temporal rather than cultic tasks.[6] In biblical Greek the term is used freely, rather than for any defined office (Neh 11:9; 2 Kings 11:15; 1 Macc 1:51).

An interesting parallel to later church use of the title is found among the Essenes, where the Hebrew word, *mebaqqer,* was a technical designation of an important officer and teacher in the community. He watched over the admission of candidates to the community (1 QS 6:12-14; CD 13:7-13), dealt with transgressions (CD 9:16-20; 14:9-10), received and distributed gifts (CD 14:12-16). Outside of Qumran and the Essene documents, *mebaqqer* is translated *episcopos.* However, without showing some parallel functions between the *episkopoi* at Philippi and the *mebaqqerim* at Qumran, it would be risky to use the Essene office as the proper background in which to understand the Philippian office.

---

[5]H.Beyer, "episkeptomai, ktl.," *Theological Dictionary of the New Testament,* II, 609; for the function in the government of Athens cf. esp. Plutarch, *Life of Solon,* XIX, 2.

[6]For references, cf. Beyer, "episkeptomai, ktl.," p. 612-61; H. Lietzmann, "Zur altchristlichen Verfassungsgeschichte," *Zeitschrift fuer wissenschaftliche Theologie,* 55 (1914), 97-153.

Episkopos is not a term otherwise used by Paul, hence, one that seems to have developed in the Philippian church. For its meaning, we can say few things for sure. In this text the name *episkopoi* with that of *diakonoi* seems to point to a rather generalized activity of oversight and service. The two positions were specific enough for Paul to single the groups out for greeting. Yet Paul uses no definite articles with these titles. He is not addressing "the bishops" or "the deacons" at Philippi. Rather Paul directly addresses the whole church of Philippi, simply mentioning bishops and deacons. Paul refers to these people by the plural nouns. The *episkopos* and *diakonos* form part of a group rather than functioning as dominant individuals. Neither here nor elsewhere in Paul's letters does this group function like the *episkopoi-presbyteroi* of Acts 20:28, that is, as some representative body of governing elders, nor does it function like groups of the same name in 1 Tim 3:2 and Tit 1:7, who operate as a body of authoritative teachers presiding over the local church as a head presides over his household.

We thus see a whole cluster of terms referring to administrative functions. The various names and descriptions all suggest basic material support and management within the community. Someone or some group had to provide a place or places for the assemblies. Someone had to provide room and board for the traveling brethren, to provide funds for traveling, or even be free enough to do the traveling. When Paul speaks of the need for order in the assembly, he must have had some one or some group in mind who could establish this necessary order. At times someone may have had to appear in court or otherwise represent the community to civil authorities, even to the extent of posting bail (cf. Acts 17:9). All of these functions describe the work of local leaders and administrators.

The very variety of titles and descriptions used to designate this group suggests the strong influence of local circumstances in bringing about their definition. Nothing is ever said about Paul or anyone else in the church appointing or instituting such leaders. This silence is particularly important where Paul goes out of his way to strengthen the authority of some persons who are in fact leaders in the community.

> You know the household of Stephanas ... I urge you to submit yourselves to such people (1 Cor 16:15-16).

> We ask you, brothers, to recognize those ... presiding over you in the Lord (1 Thess 5:12).

At such times a reminder of any special appointment or ordination would have been very appropriate. Apparently, then, the precise manner in which a person became a leader was not a concern for Paul. We are, therefore, led to suspect that the social forces of the time and culture did in fact provide for their emergence.

The group that comes to mind as the one that could easily emerge in this manner with these responsibilities are the heads of household, men and women with the means and the ability to manage the affairs of the church. In general they would have been persons of some education and a relatively broad background. Especially in the larger households, these persons would have had considerable administrative experience.

These persons would have been those who opened their homes to a church assembly. They would be the leading members in every house church, directing their household in assembly much as they did during "normal" periods of household life. They would have been the hosts for others who attached themselves to their household church. One of them would have been the host to "the whole church" for the assembly of the Christians of a city.

In the absence of Paul, everything favored the emergence of the host as the most influential member at the Lord's supper and hence the most likely presider. He or she would have provided the place for assembly as well as the food for those that did not bring their own. He or she would have decided when to begin. When Paul writes about abuses at the Lord's supper, he appears to be addressing the hosts, the only ones who could assure the order Paul wants.

> Therefore, my brothers, when you gather for the eating [of the Lord's supper], wait for one another. If one is hungry, let him eat at home (1 Cor 11:33-34).

The fact that Paul never explicitly mentions any such special leaders at Christian assembly is significant.The rigorous assignment of roles and places was simply not an issue for Paul and in the Pauline church. Nowhere even remotely do we find any concern for a "validly ordained" or otherwise officially recognized minister, whose presence and action was vital for the assembly "to work." It is precisely in the absence of such a concern on the part of Paul, that we should presume a presiding role for the host, man or woman, the head of the household who becomes the patron for the assembly.

The choice of the household head as presider at the Lord's Supper fits well into what we know about Paul's social attitudes. Paul clearly respects the hierarchy of the household, a pecking order which was taken very seriously by society. Paul's instructions regarding slaves, children, and dependent women show the basic acceptance of the household order. Paul's instructions about the silence of married women in church is an intrusion of that pecking order into his view of church order (1 Cor 14:33b-36). The social order apparently demanded (*aischron gar estin*) decent women to refrain from entering into public conversation with men during such a meeting.[7]

In this respect Paul has been labeled a social conservative. He attempts to bring about conversion by infusing love within the structures of society, not by changing the structures. The slave is to remain a slave, but obey in love. The master is to remain a master, but to see his slave as his brother in Christ. This "love patriarchalism," as it has been called,[8] accepts the authoritative role of the head of the household and the cor-

---

[7]Cf. Sallust's description of courtesans in such a setting, Sallust, *Bellum Catilinae,* XXIII, 3-4; XXVII, 2.

[8]Cf. E. Troelitch, *The Social Teaching of the Christian Churches,* trans. O.Wyon (New York: 1931), I, 69-89;G.Theissen, *Social Setting.,* pp. 107-110.

responding submission of the other members as the cohesive force in this basic unit of society.

4. Building Up the Body

As applied to church, the household order undergoes a particular transformation in the hands of Paul. This transformation from within moves in the general line of an openness to the local and wider church, conceived especially as "the body of Christ."

Paul urges all the various roles within the church to work together "advantageously" (*pros to sympheron,* 1 Cor 12:7). Given the stress of Paul on this point, we can suspect serious difficulties existed, or at least the potential for serious difficulties existed, for this type of advantageous cooperation to occur.

In effect two sources of administrative authority existed in the Pauline churches. On the one hand, the hosts and patrons literally had the "power of the keys." On the other hand, "apostles, prophets, and teachers" could speak as interpreters of divine will. The host-patrons were linked to the house church. The apostles, prophets, and teachers represented the larger church.

Later writings will show evidence of conflict between these two types of authorities. Diotrephes, apparently the powerful head of a house church, opposes the authority of "the elder" and his traveling emissaries (3 Jn 9-10). The Didache speaks of the testing of itinerant teachers, apostles, and prophets by the local leaders who have the authority to accord or refuse hospitality to any teacher, prophet, or apostle not meeting the established criteria (ch. 11-13). The Didache also speaks of the local "bishops and deacons" assuming the ministry of "prophets and teachers" (15:1).

Paul's insistence on the priority of apostles, prophets, and teachers may indicate a need to insist on their importance. To the degree these were traveling officers, like Paul himself, they would arrive in a city church without assets and without special friends to provide political support, a position of weakness with which Paul was familiar. The itinerant apostles, prophets, and teachers likewise could easily appear as a disruptive influence in the local church and in the house churches. Later 2 Timothy will have unkind things to say against those "who worm their way into households and make captives of silly women" (3:6).

On the other hand the lack of special honorific titles for host-patrons in the Pauline churches stands in stark contrast to the counterparts in non-Christians associations, both Jewish and Gentile. There is no "father of the church" or "mother of the church" here in virtue of being a major benefactor. The titles typical of the associations, *archontes, tamias, epistatai, hegemones, ktl.,* are all absent from the Pauline communities. It was all work and no play for the Christian administrators, who may have wondered why their non-Christian peers could enjoy extravagant positions of respect. In a short time, the presbyter-bishop will have assumed the teaching role and become a person with a "noble task" (1 Tim 3:1-7; Tit 1:5-9).

We must, however, be careful of reading a later situation into the Corinthian church. The difficulty in Corinth is actually not with overreaching "administrators," but with the spectacular gifts overshadowing others more important for "the building up" of the Church. The only gift Paul seems intent on keeping in its place is that of "kinds of tongues," which he consistently places at the end of the lists and explicitly subordinates to the gift of "prophecy."

With the analogy of the body (1 Cor 12:12-27), framed by the double list of gifts (12:8-10 and 12:28-30), Paul insists on the mutuality of the gifts. No one function can place itself above the body. In fact any special honor bestowed on a role is by that fact an indication of its lower status (12:23-24). Paul appears to be countering a tendency toward a hierarchy of honor in Corinth, although the hierarchy he is opposing appears to be based on miraculous rather than administrative power.

If anything Paul seems disappointed with the "leaders" in Corinth. They are not maintaining the necessary order of the

Lord's supper (1 Cor 11). They are not functioning as the arbitrators of disputes among the brethren (1 Cor 6). They are not maintaining moral discipline (1 Cor 5). All indications point to a lack of development of these local patron-authorities. They are not yet representing the church to outside authorities. They are evidently not in charge of any central church fund, since Paul asks each person in the Corinthian church to put aside some money each week by himself (*par' heautō*, 1 Cor 16:2). We see in this church the slow development of a working authority.

Paul's response to any deficiencies of leadership or any other office is always the same. It is not to bolster the office with an infusion of authority, but rather to remind the local church of its role as "the body of Christ." For Paul the roles of any of the leaders is not qualitatively different from that of the body as a whole. The tasks of the leaders are the same Paul assigns to the body. Prophets, for instance, have the task of "building up" (*oikodomē* 1 Cor 14:3), but so does every Christian have this task (1 Cor 8:1; 1 Thess 5:11). Leaders are to "admonish" (*nouthetein*, 1 Thess 5:12), but so are all the members (1 Thess 5:14). Prophets are to give "encouragement" and "comfort" (*paraklēsis, paramythia*, 1 Cor 14:3) which is the responsibility of all (2 Cor 13:11; 1 Thess 5:14).

Such a parallelism of tasks does not deny the existence of specialized ministries in Paul's mind, it simply points out the basic solidarity of "the body" as prior to any distinguishing of roles. Thus even the household "pecking order" could not function the same as in a non-Christian household, at least not while the household was *en ekklēsia*. Despite inconsistencies in his instructions, Paul would eventually state this principle clearly:

> For those baptized into Christ, you have clothed yourself with Christ. There is no Jew or Greek, no slave or free person, no male or female. All of you are one in Christ (Gal 3:27-28).

The need for stronger administrative leadership in the church could be taken care of by a greater sense of "the body." Such leadership would be read in terms of a special gift of the same Spirit who empowers others to work miracles or prophesy and who provides everyone with their special gift. The patron-leader would find satisfaction in his or her role for the body under the Spirit. No special human honors would be needed; no division between clergy and laity.

Even the manner of leadership would be governed by a sense of "the body." Reciprocity would be the tone of direction, not commands from above. Discernment, interpretation, and testing by the community would be the counterpart of even the most important form of leadership. We see this tone in Paul's urging, "exhorting," even "begging," terms which far outweigh any "commanding." We find this tone in the role of the community "to test" (*dokimazein*) the prophets (1 Thess 5:21) and in the need of the community "to recognize" (*eidenai*) the leadership of men like Stephanas (1 Cor 16:15).

The sense of being "the body of Christ," as we have seen (chapter 1), carried the Christian beyond the house church, even beyond the local church, to the perspective of a world-wide people. A house church closed on itself would lose that perspective, and the deformity we see in 3 John would naturally arise, a patriarchalism in which power and "love of being first" becomes an end in itself (v. 9).

5

The Gathering

The Corinthian correspondence is our main source for understanding what went on at a Christian gathering. The data, however, is fragmentary mostly because Paul did not need to describe the details of the assembly to his readers. Rather, he had to deal with problems. Nor does Paul anywhere tell us clearly about assembly activities specific to the house churches as different from those of local churches. Barring any information that would allow us to distinguish between the two assemblies, we must suppose that the two types of assemblies basically functioned the same way. Except for activities related to the size of the assembly and the availability of the full range of gifted persons, the house church, we must assume, did the same things as the local church.

The two most important descriptions of the Christian assembly, those in 1 Cor 11:17-34, and 1 Cor 14. Both describe city-wide meetings. Dealing with the Lord's Supper, Paul begins, "When you come together in the same place" (*synerchomenōn oun hymōn epi to auto,* 1 Cor 11:20). Speaking of the exercises of tongues and prophecy, Paul explicitly refers to "the whole church (*hē ekklēsia holē*) coming together in the same place" (1 Cor 14:23). In both references, however, Paul has a specific reason for dealing with the city church. For the Lord's Supper, Paul wants to deal with the problem of rich and poor coming together, a situation virtually inevitable for a city-wide assembly and one less likely to occur in the house church. For the tongues and prophecy assembly, Paul wants to picture an outsider's reaction to the two forms of activity. Again such a situation would be more likely to occur at the large gathering of the local church than in the privacy of a house church. Because Paul thus describes the Lord's Supper and the celebration of the gifts at the level of the local church, we cannot immediately conclude that those types of celebrations occurred only on that level.

1. The Lord's Supper

On the contrary, the details of Paul's description of the Lord's Supper, especially when contrasted with later descriptions of the ritualized Eucharist, strongly suggest the individual household as the normal environment. Paul describes a full meal. His expression for celebrating the Lord's Supper is *kyriakon deipnon phagein*. The Greek word *deipnon* indicates a main meal, usually in the evening (cf. Lk 14:12; Jn 13:4; 21:20).The word describing participating in this supper is the normal word for "eating," *phagein* (aorist of *esthiō*, cf. Rom 14:2; 1 Cor 10:27; Lk 10:8). In contrast Justin writing about a century later, describes participating in the now ritualized Eucharist as *metalepsis*, "sharing."[1]

The entire focus of Paul is on the manner of eating, and specifically how the Christians relate to each other in this eating. He is concerned about who goes hungry and who fills up. Later descriptions of Eucharist focus almost entirely on the manner in which an official is "to conduct the Eucharist" (*eucharistein, Didache*, 9-10; Justin *1 Apology*, 67). Paul is completely silent about any regular presider or official at this event. In contrast, the Didache around the 90s speaks of prophets offering Eucharist (10:7) and Justin refers to "the president" (*ho proestōs*) as the one who prays over the bread and wine.[2]

[1] *1 Apology,* 67,5.
[2] *1 Apology,* 67,5.

Even the action with the bread and wine recalls a family meal in a Jewish home. Breaking and distributing bread was a normal way of beginning a meal in a Jewish home of the time, just as sharing a cup of wine was the usual way of ending a meal. For each gesture special blessings were said.[3] In effect it becomes difficult to visualize how such a meal could have taken place with a group as large as "the whole church." Even supposing a very large dining room and a very generous host, we are faced with logistic problems most people are willing to face only on special occasions.

Once the Lord's Supper became a stylized meal, with a chip of bread and a sip of wine, a weekly gathering of a large group became feasible. Justin does in fact speak of a ritualized weekly eucharistic gathering, a blessing and a sharing of bread and wine without any accompanying meal "on the Day of the Sun."[4] By Justin's time, the Eucharist had been separated from the Supper.

A weekly "Lord's Supper" or "Breaking of Bread," however, appears much earlier. Acts speaks of Paul at Troas "gathering on the first day of the week to break bread" (20:7). Other early texts speak of Christians celebrating on this day.[5]

In Paul the only allusion to a weekly rhythm to the Christian's life is found in his instructions about collection for the church of Jerusalem:

> On the first [day] of the week let each of you put aside by himself (*par heautō*) in savings something of what you have gained (1 Cor 16:2).

The text implies some special Christian activity on Sunday. Given the later connection of this day with Eucharist, we can suppose with some probability that Paul has in mind a week-

---

[3]Cf. J. Jeremias, *The Eucharistic Words of Jesus* (New York: Scribners, 1966), p. 35; Mishnah, *Berakoth*, 6:1; Jer 16:7.

[4]*1 Apology*, 67,3.

[5]*Barnabas*, 15:9; cf. Ignatius, *Magnesians*, 9,1: Revelation 1:10.

ly Lord's Supper. Since he refers to an "installment plan" operating for each "by himself," not one involving "the whole church," Paul most likely is thinking of the individual house churches, not the city church, as the occasion during which this regular contribution takes place.

If there was a weekly Lord's Supper, then, it most likely was in the individual household church. Special occasions would have called for a gathering of the whole church for this celebration, such as Paul directly addresses in 1 Corinthians 11.

Nevertheless a real tendency toward larger gatherings for the Lord's Supper appears in Paul's interpretation of the meaning of this action:

> The cup of blessing which we bless, is it not an association (*koinōnia*) in the blood of Christ? The bread which we break, is it not an association (*koinōnia*) in the body of Christ? Because there is one bread, we though many are one body. All of us partake of the one bread (1 Cor 10:16-17).

Paul sees this action as an activity and a realization of the unity of the body of Christ. Paul draws up this picture by the contrast between "the many" and "the one." The more included in "the many," the more dramatic becomes the realization of "the one." It is to the whole Corinthian church that Paul addresses the words, "You are the body of Christ" (1 Cor 12:27). It would seem, therefore, he has in mind the whole Corinthian church as involved in the blessing of the cup and the breaking of the bread.

The example of their Jewish and Gentile neighbors may have encouraged the early Christians to develop the city-wide meal. While the principal feasts were celebrated by meals in the Jewish household, special occasions like circumcisions, betrothals, weddings, and funerals often involved celebrations in the form of meals actually in the synagogue, evidently involving large numbers of persons. Outside of the synagogue common meals of Jewish associations or *haburot* brought members together. At Qumran the common meal held twice a day and presided over by a priest had clear cultic tones.[6] Even more so among Gentile associations, festive meals were a common feature. The dining room was a distinctive and regular feature of the cult centers. Cult members attended the sacred meals as though invited by the god. The sacred meal was particularly important at the moment of initiation into the mysteries of the cult.[7] Paul in fact draws an explicit contrast between sharing in the sacred meal of a pagan rite and sharing in the Lord's Supper:

> You cannot drink the cup of the Lord and the cup of demons. You cannot have part in the table of the Lord and the table of demons (1 Cor 10:21).

This contrast, which he expects his readers to understand, would be clearest if Paul and his readers were thinking of the city-wide Lord's supper.

Still the logistic problems remain. Jews had the synagogue building as a place for meals with large numbers; Gentiles had their temples. Such facilities, however, were precisely what the Christians lacked. Hence, the city-wide Lord's Supper was probably held only on special occasions.

2. Sharing the Gifts

Paul's other major reference to the Christian gathering describes the activity of sharing the gifts of the Spirit:

[6]1 QS 6:20-21.

[7]Cf. Apuleius, *The Golden Ass*, XI, 24-25; Josephus, *Jewish Antiquities*, XVIII, 73.

When you gather, let each one have a psalm, a teaching, a revelation, a tongue, an interpretation. Let it all take place for edification (1 Cor 14:26).

Paul then gives precise instructions regarding tongues and prophecy along with their corresponding gifts of interpretation and discernment (14:26-33.37-40).

The reference to "a psalm" may allude to the Christian use of the Jewish psalter, or it may indicate the development of Christian compositions. Col 3:16 speaks of "psalms, hymns, and spiritual songs" by which Christians taught and admonished each other as well as praised God. Christian poetic compositions have in fact been identified in the New Testament, such as those in Phil 2:6-22 or Col 1:15-20.

The "teaching" must have included stories about Jesus as well as the development of a Christian code of morality. Whereas "a revelation" probably involved apocalyptic type predictions of things to come as well as the dramatic presentation of "a word of the Lord" (cf. 1 Cor 7:12.25).

The number of Old Testament citations in the letters of Paul give us a clue to the importance of Scripture in the Pauline churches. Scriptural interpretation was probably the turf of "the teacher" (cf. the example of Apollos, Acts 18:24). Full-blown scriptural homilies can be identified in Paul's very letters, for example 1 Cor 1:18-2:16 or Rom 4:1-25.[8] Composed prior to the letters in which they are found, these homilies most likely were delivered to church assemblies as exercises of Paul's gift of teaching.

A "tongue" and its "interpretation" formed part of the prayers of the community. Whether in the ecstatic form of "tongues" or in the communicable form of intelligent speech, prayer must have occupied a large part of the Christian gathering. Paul's letters echo "blessings" (2 Cor 1:3-7), "doxo-

---

[8]Cf. V. Branick, "Source and Redaction Criticism of 1 Cor 1-3," *JBL*, 101 (1982), 251-69.

logies" (Rom 7:25; 16:25-27; 1 Cor 15:57), as well as the Aramaic acclamations that stemmed from the earliest Christians (Gal 1:5; 1 Cor 16:22; Rom 8:15).

In 1 Corinthians 14 Paul dwells on the exercise of both "tongues" and "prophecy" during the Christian assembly. We get the impression from Paul's emphasis that "tongues" and "prophecy" occupied an important place in the Corinthian assembly. The rules for order apply in a particular way to the city-wide assembly, "Let two or three prophets speak, and let the others discern" (14:29). The private house-church need hardly worry about such an abundance of prophets.

On the other hand, his instructions about prophecy in 1 Cor 11:2-16 might concern primarily the exercise of this gift in the private house church. His comments on the city-wide gathering begin explicitly only at 11:17. In the preceding verses Paul deals with both men and women prophesying, in apparent and baffling contradiction to his later prohibition against women speaking in church (14:33-36). The more drastic resolution to this contradiction is to see 14:33-36 as a later addition to the letter. An alternative could be to see the earlier instruction about women prophets as dealing with activities in the private house church.

Whether in the private house church or the city-wide gathering, the orientation of the assembly was praising God while teaching or admonishing one another. Building up the body was the goal of this gathering and the norm of its functions. The interaction among believers reflected the interaction between God and the believer. The family language of kinship which described the bonds among believers paralleled the family language describing the love of God for his people, the love of a father for his children (Rom 8:14.16.19.21; 9:8.26; 1 Cor 8:6; Phil 2:15; Gal 3:26-4:8).

This social orientation distinguished the Christian gathering from its Jewish and pagan counterparts. The focus for the Jewish assembly was the Torah. The blessings, the readings, the prayers, and the instructions all oriented the assembly toward understanding the Law and working out its

practical consequences in *hallachah,* the "way of walking."[9]
On the other hand the focus for the pagan assembly was cult.
Dominating these assemblies were the processions, the
dances, the dramatic rituals, and the sacred meals of com-
munion with gods.[10]

The Christian gatherings under Paul may not have even
looked like a religion to an outsider. The Christians had no
shrines, temples, cult statues, priests, or sacrifices. For Christians, Paul writes, the community is the temple:

> Do you not know that you are the temple of God (*naos
> theou*) and the Spirit of God dwells in you?.... The
> temple of God is holy. You are precisely that (1 Cor
> 3:16-17).

One's whole life makes up worship and sacrifice:

> I beseech you, brothers, through the mercies of God, pre-
> sent your bodies as a living sacrifice (*thysian*), holy (*hag-
> ian*) and pleasing to God, as your spiritual worship (*la-
> treian*). Do not conform to this world, but be transformed
> by a renewal of mind, in order to test what the will of God
> is, what is good and pleasing and perfect (Rom 12:1-2).

The language of cult is there—"sacrifice," "holy," "worship."
But Paul has reinterpreted it—in a way not dissimilar from
the prophets—so that cult is not clearly distinguished from
daily life.

The Christian gathering as a sharing of gifts, as an exercise
in mutual "edification," was for Paul, then, an act of worship.
Sacred space was not an issue. The assembly was its own
sanctuary. Hence even the family dining room was an appropriate place for church.

---

[9]Cf. Philo, *On the Embassy to Gaius,* 156; *On Dreams,* II, 127; *Moses,* II, 215-16;
Josephus, *Jewish War,* II, 301; *Jewish Antiquities,* XIX, 300.305; Mishnah, *Megil-
lah,* 3-4; *Sotah,* 7:7-8; *Aboth,* 1:1-2.

[10]Cf. Apuleius, *The Golden Ass,* XI; Plutarch, *On Isis and Osiris,* 2-4.

Were these "sharing the gift" assemblies distinct from the "Lord's Supper" assemblies? Paul treats them separately in his discussion of the needed reforms, and he never speaks about a transition from one type of activity to the other. The principal argument for seeing two separate assemblies for the two types of church activities rests on another issue, namely the degree in which the Lord's supper excluded outsiders. We must first examine this issue.

3. Exclusivity at the Assemblies?

Paul makes mention of the presence of outsiders at the "gifts assemblies," at least those involving tongues and prophecies:

> If the whole church is gathered together in the same place and all are speaking in tongues, would not an outsider or an unbeliever who enters think you are all out of your minds. If, however, all are prophesying, an unbeliever or an outsider would be accused by all and examined by all.... Such a one would fall on his face and worship God, proclaiming, "Surely God is with you" (1 Cor 14:23-25).

Would Paul or the Corinthians have wanted outsiders at the Lord's Supper, where the solidarity or "body" of Christians appeared to be the objective of the service and the norm of its conduct? The *Didache* clearly expresses the closed nature of the "Eucharist" of the 90s:

> Let none eat or drink of your Eucharist except those baptized in the name of the Lord. For about this the Lord has spoken. "Give not what is holy to pigs" (9:5).

If we read this exclusivity into the Corinthian "Lord's Suppers" at the time of Paul, we must see such an assembly as meeting separately from the "gifts assembly." The question at hand is basically how Paul drew the boundaries for the

Christian association.

It may, however, be a distortion of Paul's attitude to read back this "eucharistic exclusivity," for which we have no evidence prior to the Didache. While Paul's emphasis on the solidarity of Christians expressed in the Lord's Supper may in fact logically lead to excluding outsiders, this "logical conclusion" could also be applied to the "gifts assembly" where Paul also strongly emphasized the unity and "body" of the Christians.

The only exclusion Paul associates with the Lord's Supper is an exclusion of idolatry:

> You cannot drink the cup of the Lord and the cup of demons. You cannot share the table of the Lord and the table of demons (1 Cor 10:21).

Dealing with meals in general, Paul speaks also of excluding a member of the community as a means of correcting immorality.

> If one who bears the title brother is immoral, covetous, an idolater, an abusive person, a drunkard, or a thief, do not eat with such a one (1 Cor 5:11).

Qualifying these instructions immediately before and immediately afterwards, however, Paul points out that he is not intending this discipline for outsiders (5:10.12).

The Gospel traditions recall the particular emphasis of Jesus' own "table fellowship." These traditions tell the stories of Jesus eating with sinners and tax collectors (cf. Mk 2:15-17) and relate the parables about the Great Banquet which would include all, even sinners (Matt 22:1-10; Lk 14:15-24). The approach of Jesus stands in contrast to the Pharisaic understanding of table fellowship as a gathering of the equally pure.[11] These traditions likewise include stories of

---

[11]Cf. Jacob Neusner, *From Politics to Piety. The Emergence of Pharisaic Judaism* (New York: KTAV, 1973).

Jesus resisting his disciples' attempts to close their circle, to draw boundaries showing clearly who was inside and who was outside (Mk 9:38-40; 10:13-16).

It is difficult to judge the influence of such traditions on Pauline Christianity which shows many signs of boundaries. Besides emphasizing the incompatibility of the Lord's Supper with idolatry (1 Cor 10:21), Paul also stresses the singularity and distinctiveness of Christians. They are "to judge the world"; hence interaction with pagan courts is inappropriate (1 Cor 6:1-11).

On the other hand, as we have seen, the Pauline church did not exclude the outsider from its meetings (1 Cor 14:23). General social relationships like those involving meals with non-Christians may have posed some serious difficulties, but were accepted as normal (1 Cor 10:23-33). Erastos, the city treasurer of Corinth, would certainly have had to kiss his job goodbye were he unable to associate in a whole range of meals and other activities with his pagan peers. Even the intimate relationship of marriage not only was possible between Christian and non-Christian but was a way of "making holy" the non-Christian partner (1 Cor 7:12-16). While Paul spoke of sin and evil on a cosmic scale, he did not fear contamination from the world (1 Cor 5:10) and did not include political authority in this evil sphere. Paul saw civil rulers in fact as agents of God (Rom 13:1-7).

The Pauline church thus lived in a complex relationship with pagan society. Boundaries were clearly drawn in that members were distinguished from non-members. But nothing in Paul comes close to the exclusivity of Pharisaism or even that of Johannine Christianity. Paul stresses a basic missionary thrust toward all people.

> Admonishing everyone and teaching everyone in all wisdom, in order to present everyone perfect in Christ (Col 1:28).

He looks forward to a reconciliation of all humanity (Rom 11:25-32).

While Paul may have welcomed the privacy of the household, nothing indicates that he was seeking secrecy or even
separation from outsiders. If the Lord's Supper symbolized
the cohesiveness of Christians as the body of Christ, it did
not necessarily symbolize an exclusivity with outsiders. Paul
does not manifest the same radical openness we have in
Jesus, but there is no reason to think that Paul would have
any more problems with an outsider being present at the
Lord's Supper than he would with such a person present at
the exercise of tongues and prophecy.

4. One or Two Assemblies?

If the argument concerning outsiders does not demand
our seeing two assemblies for the Lord's Supper and for the
sharing of the gifts, do we have any indication of both activities occurring in one assembly? While Paul does not explicitly relate the two activities, his parallel use of words in
dealing with the two does in fact suggest their close connection. The term "to gather," *synerchesthai,* is used for the
Lord's Supper (1 Cor 11:17.18.20.33.34) and for the sharing
of the gifts (1 Cor 14:23.26). Forcefully disagreeing with the
Corinthians Paul writes,

> When you gather in the same place, it is not to eat the
> Lord's supper, because each of you rushes to take your
> own supper (1 Cor 11:20).

The strength of Paul's rebuke depends on the presupposition
on the part of the Corinthians, namely, when they did gather
epi to auto, it was their intention to eat the Lord's Supper.
Paul, however, tells the same group,

> When you gather, let each have a psalm, have a teaching,
> have a revelation, have a tongue, or have an interpreta-
> tion. Let all happen for edification (1 Cor 14:26).

Another verbal parallel can be found in the very terms *eu-*

charistein, eucharistia, which were rapidly joining the technical vocabulary for referring to the Lord's Supper (Matt 26:27; Mk 26:27; Lk 22:17.19; cf. Mk 15:36; Jn 6:11; Acts 27:35). Paul describes the Last Supper tradition with the verb form (1 Cor 11:24), but he also uses this vocabulary with remarkable frequency in the discussion of prophecy and tongues (1 Cor 14:16-18).

It is the theme of "the body" (*ho soma*) that particularly links the Lord's Supper with the sharing of the gifts. The whole discussion of the organic unity of the diverse gifts centers around Paul's identification of the assembly as "the body of Christ" (12:12-30, esp. 12:27). The "body of Christ" is in fact the gathering of Christians, who all "have been watered by the same Spirit" and thus have been incorporated by baptism into this body (12:13), who then as gifted with diverse powers and roles need each other and care for each other (12:21.25).

Paul earlier roots the establishment of the "one body" with participating in the Lord's Supper. Christians are one body because (*gar*) they partake of the one bread (10:17). Without trying to give his readers any precise sacramental theology, Paul plays with the thought-provoking ambiguity of the term "body of Christ." Twice he refers to the body of Christ in connection with the blood of Christ:

> The cup of blessing which we bless, is it not a sharing in the blood of Christ? The bread we break, is it not a sharing in the body of Christ? (10:16).

> Thus whoever eats the bread or drinks the cup of the Lord unworthily sins against the body and blood of the Lord (11:27).

By these references he is thinking of the historical body given for us and the historical blood in which the new covenant was sealed (11:24-25). Immediately after this allusion to the body and blood, Paul then drops any further reference to the blood and speaks of "the body" as the gathering of Christians:

Because the bread is one, we though many are one body (10:17).

He who eats and drinks without recognizing the body is eating and drinking judgment on himself (11:29).

The first example of this shift is clear from the wording, "we," that is, all those gathering to partake of the one bread, "are one body." The second example is not as clear. Later dogmatic theology, searching for "Real Presence" theology in Scripture texts, read "the body" in 11:29 as the body of Jesus in the Eucharist. It is unlikely, however that Paul would suddenly and without explanation flash adherence to a dogmatic teaching as the criterion for eating and drinking at the Lord's Supper. Paul's focus up to this point has been the Corinthians' reprehensible attitude at the Lord's Supper which consisted in failure to observe the unity of the assembly (11:18-22). "Recognizing the body" in this context means recognizing that those who partake of the one bread are one body.

Nevertheless, as following upon the preceding reference to the "body and blood of the Lord," the phrase "recognizing the body" necessarily creates an ambiguity, a lack of precision in which the assembly, the bread, and the historical body of Jesus tend to blur together. This blurriness, in fact, is Paul's way of drawing essential connections. By poetic evocation, Paul is saying that the one body of Christ, which the Christians together form, cannot be separated from the Lord's Supper, just as the worthy eating of the Lord's Supper depends on the unity of the body.

If Paul then appeals to the unity of the body as the guiding idea for the proper sharing of gifts, it seems likely that he expected the sharing of the gifts and the Lord's Supper to go together. If the two types of activities went together at the same gathering, most likely the sharings of prophecy, teachings, tongues and other services of the word followed that of the Lord's Supper. The hint we have of this comes from those who arrived late and had nothing to eat (1 Cor 11:21.33). If the meal followed the "word service," as is often supposed, then these people would be late for everything. Paul wants the Corinthians to wait before starting, that is, before beginning to eat the Lord's Supper (1 Cor 11:21.33). Such an order would have its parallel in the procedures of philosophical symposiums. Here the members would begin with a common meal. The passing around of a drink then signaled the moment to pass from eating to philosophical discussion.[12]

If we connect the Lord's Supper and sharing the gifts, then we probably should expect both types of activity together also in the house church assembly, even though the whole range of gifts would be seen only in the city-wide assembly. The house church would have its "gifted administrator." This would probably be the head of the house, the patron of the house church. If the household were lucky, it might also have a gifted healer, teacher, or prophet.

5. Other Assemblies

BAPTISM

Along with the Lord's Supper, baptism appears in Paul as one of the "official actions" of church. In the opening chapters of 1 Corinthians, Paul refers several times to baptism (1:13-17), mentioning how he personally baptized Crispus and Gaius along with the house of Stephanas (1:14-16), but that his mission was to preach, not to baptize (1:17). He is worried about factions arising among the Corinthians from an overemphasis on the person administering baptism (1:13).

Christian baptism is specifically a baptism "into Christ" (Gal 3:27; Rom 6:3), which, Paul explains, is a baptism "into his death." It is a way of "being buried with Christ" (Rom 6:3; Col 2:12). For Paul baptism is likewise a baptism "into one body," an incorporation into that diverse and organic

[12]Klauck, *Hausgemeinde,* p. 37.

unity which is the church with all the gifts of its members, "Jew or Greek, slave or free." Christians are baptized "in the Spirit," for baptism is "being watered with the one Spirit" (1 Cor 12:13).

The ritual we see here, which has its roots in Jewish prose-lyte baptism, is an action for outsiders. Like preaching, baptism involves not so much the interaction of Christians as rather the missionary activity of Christians toward non-believers.

An exception would be the "baptism for the dead," to which Paul briefly refers without providing any further de-tails (1 Cor 15:29). Such an action sounds like that of an assembly of Christians apparently for the benefit of dead relatives or friends. We hear of this "baptism for the dead" only in Corinth.

The comparisons made between baptism and entering the tomb of Christ suggest immersion under water. This does not sound like the activity that could take place at a house church or even at the meeting of the city church at a house. The house impluvium—the small pool in the courtyard—would be only a few feet deep. Furthermore an assembly of this sort might not be the appropriate place for the nudity generally involved in baptism.

To my knowledge the earliest indications we have of a setting for Christian baptism come from Justin, some one hundred years after Paul. Writing about the practice in Rome, Justin mentions the preliminary instructions and communal prayers and fasting.

> Then they are led by us to where there is water, and they are reborn in the same manner of regeneration by which we ourselves have been reborn. For they are then given washing in the water in the name of God the father and master of all, of our saviour Jesus Christ, and of the Holy Spirit.[13]

[13] *1 Apology*, 61,3.

This place "where there is water" may be the public bath, over which, according to Justin, the church of Rome assembled.[14] When the Didache allows for different kinds of water in which to baptize and specifically describes pouring water on the head of the new Christian, it does not indicate any place where this is to happen. Baptism by pouring, however, could allow baptism to take place in church. By the third century, rooms will be designed in churches specifically for baptisms, such as that in the church of Dura-Europos.

THE DISCIPLINARY MEETING

Writing to the Corinthians, Paul speaks also of a special church gathering to deal with disciplining a member. A Corinthian having sexual relations with his step-mother is to be punished in some form of exclusion from the community. Instead of accepting this breach of morality with self-satisfaction, the Corinthian church should have taken care of this and now must do something:

> For I, absent in body but present in the Spirit, have—as in fact present (*hos parōn*)—already decided in the name of our Lord Jesus, while you and my spirit assemble (*synachthentōn*), to hand over the one acting in such a way to Satan for the destruction of his body in order that [his] spirit be saved in the day of the Lord (1 Cor 5:3-5).

Apparently avoiding the word *ekklēsia* or the usual verb to describe a church gathering, *synerchomai*, Paul refers here to a special assembly to deal with disciplinary matters. This assembly was an exercise in the local community's responsibility for self-discipline. When the group assembles, however, Paul warns that he too will be present in spirit, and "in fact

---

[14] *Passio sancti Justini et socii*, 3.3.

present" has already passed judgment on the matter. We have here, thus, an important indication of an openness of the local community to an even wider form of authority, namely Paul's.

Another disciplinary meeting, dealing with an apparently unrelated case, is also implied in 2 Cor 2:5-11, where Paul urges clemency on some Corinthian who has seriously offended him, since a punishment has already been inflicted "by the majority" (*hoi pleiones*). Paul seems to be referring to the main body of the Corinthian church. As with the other disciplinary meeting, we seem to have a special assembly.

In both these texts the special assembly clearly involves the life of the city-wide church. Such disciplinary matters would be out of the hands of a house church. Paul is addressing the Corinthians as a whole when he tells them either to be severe or to be lenient. Paul speaks of a group, *hoi pleiones,* that has already meted out punishment to an adversary of Paul. Although the comparative form, *hoi pleiones* ("the more"), is not as all-inclusive as the positive form, *hoi polloi,* ("the many"), the context of Paul's description suggests the meaning of "the rest of the congregation" in contrast to the one being punished. That is, Paul seems to be referring to a unanimous decision. The local Pauline church was then to have the power over its members to inflict discipline, probably in some form of excommunication.

A type of city-wide assembly may be implied in Paul's instructions to the Corinthians to settle legal disputes among themselves without recourse to civil courts (1 Cor 6:1-11). The only detail Paul gives here about this church function is the need for "someone wise among you" who can settle the disputes (6:5). The comparisons drawn with the civil courts suggests something like a public hearing, more likely a special meeting rather than the worship gathering. The very idea of litigation suggests disputes between property owners rather than matters within a household. Again we are led to picture Paul urging the city-wide church to act as a body, but outside of "church" strictly speaking.

READING THE LETTERS

Finally we must look at Paul's instructions regarding the reading of his letters:

> Greet all the brothers with a holy kiss. I adjure you by the Lord to read this letter to all the brothers (1 Thess 5:26-27).
>
> Once this letter has been read among you (*par' hymin*), see that it is read in the church of the Laodiceans and that you read [the one] from Laodicea (Col 4:16).

Paul is talking about public readings of his letters, ones which are aloud to a group of people. Does Paul expect the readings to take place in plenary assemblies of city churches or does he envision successive readings? Given the type of exchange he asks among the Colossians and Laodiceans, Paul sees nothing of special import in a gathering of all together for the reading of his letters. On the other hand, the stress on "all" the Thessalonians would seem to presuppose a plenary gathering—which may have been the only type of gathering in "the church of the Thessalonians."

Paul's vocabulary in his instructions to the Colossians likewise suggests full gatherings. To the citizens of Colossae, he asks that the letter be read, not simply "by you" or "to you," but "among you" (*par' hymin*). The preposition with the dative here expresses nearness in space, something like "at the side of." The preposition suggests the Colossians rubbing elbows as the letter is read. Similarly, the letter read "in the church of the Laodiceans" suggests a picture of all the Christian Laodiceans gathered together.

The writing of a letter by Paul to a church was special enough that we can imagine the Christians of a city eagerly gathering to hear the apostle's words. This initial reading would involve the gathering of the city-wide church that Paul has in mind in his instructions. Once, however, the letter was "officially" read, a devotional re-reading of it may have been a common practice in the house churches. 2 Peter testifies to the speed with which Paul's letters were read as one reads holy Scripture (3:15-16). The early "teachers" in both the local and the house churches could have found in Paul's words an endless source of material to interpret and explain.

6

Demise of the House Church

Soon after Paul the private house church disappears from view, and around the middle of the second century the house church as such will give way to the dedicated church building. The movement away from the house church will entail a loss of the particularly familial tone of the earliest Christian assemblies. The movement will be accompanied by major shifts in the Christian theology of church.

In this chapter we will briefly look at the beginnings of that movement. It is important, however, to see the roots of the shift already in the problems Paul had to deal with and in the approach Paul took to those problems.

1. Problems for Paul

As we have seen Paul addresses private house churches and presumes on the household to furnish much of the structure of the church, but he clearly places stress on the activity of the local or city-wide church. The city-wide church was the place where Paul tackled the problem of divisiveness, a divisiveness that seemed to have its roots in house churches.

ANTIOCH

In Antioch Jewish Christians and Gentile Christians

formed closed groups. This division shows up clearly in Paul's criticism of Peter:

> When Cephas came to Antioch, I stood up to his face because he stood condemned. He was eating with Gentiles before the arrival of some persons from James. When they arrived however be withdrew and separated himself, fearing those of the circumcision. The rest of the Jews joined in the pretense, so that even Barnabas was led away in the hypocrisy (Gal 2:11-13).

The problem here was eating together. We should most likely understand the problem as centered in the Lord's Supper (1 Cor 11:23-26). The Jews met together in Jewish houses for their eating; the Gentiles, in Gentiles houses for their eating.

The Church of Antioch, nevertheless, shows some cohesion:

> When I say that they were not walking straight toward the truth of the Gospel, I spoke to Cephas before all (*emprosthen pantōn,* Gal 2:14).

Some sort of general meeting, perhaps one dealing with discipline and order, took place even in Antioch. But this was not a Lord's Supper.

CORINTH

At Corinth divisiveness from sub-groups within the city-wide church, possibly from the house churches themselves:

> I have been informed, my brothers, by certain members of Chloe's household that there are quarrels among you. I say this because each of you say, "I am of Paul; I am of Apollos; I am of Cephas." I, however, am of Christ. Is Christ divided? (1 Cor 1:11-13)

Paul describes the divisions as *schismata* and requiring a greater agreement of thinking and judgment (1:10). We do not have full blown religious sects here based on doctrinal diversity. Paul's response to the problem does not support such an hypothesis. Rather the divisions appear more on the level of practice and a general forgetfulness of the foolishness of the cross.

Paul's remark, "I, however, am of Christ," is a sarcastic commentary on the slogans of the Corinthians. He is not describing any fourth sectarian group. This is clear from the conclusion of the section where he repeats the first three names, "whether it be Paul or Apollos or Cephas," and then proclaims, "But you are of Christ and Christ is of God" (1 Cor 3:22-23). He is describing the direct opposite of any sectarianism based on human patronage or leadership.

The point is, Christ is not divided and to be part of Christ is to be one with all other Christians in "the Church of God" (1 Cor 1:2). To be part of Christ is to form one body in him with a unity that far overshadows the pronounced autonomy of prominent families in the Hellenistic world, a unity that eclipses the activity of household heads who enjoyed authority in claiming the loyalty and solidarity of their household members.

The city-wide assembly at Corinth, however, was no automatic remedy. The problem of divisiveness also occurred at this level in the division between rich and poor. In the handling of this problem, however, Paul again seems to emphasize the nature of local church.

Poverty existed in the Church of Corinth. Despite indications of wealth and property among the Christians of Corinth (cf. chapter 3 above), Paul writes to them, "Consider your calling, brothers. Not many of you are wise in a worldly sense, not many powerful, not many well-bred" (1 Cor 1:26). These lines probably overstate the social lowliness and poverty of the Corinthian Christians. In fact Paul clearly wrote these lines along with the entire section of 1:18-2:16 for a prior audience and is inserting them now into his letter to the Corinthians.[1] However, in a city where two-thirds of the

[1]Cf.Branick, "Source and Redaction Criticism," pp. 251-69.

population were slaves, we can expect a significant number of poor and even destitute families in the church.

In effect, in the city-wide gatherings neglect of the poor vitiated the Lord's Supper. 1 Cor 11:17-34 describes the problems arising from the gathering of "the haves" and "have nots." Some arrived with plenty of food and drink and filled themselves. Others arrived with nothing and went hungry. The root of the problem was more than moral failure, it was a neglect of the very meaning of the Lord's Supper:

> Although you gather in the same place, it is not to eat the Lord's dinner (*kyriakon deipnon*). Each undertakes his own dinner (*to idion deipnon*) in this eating. So that one goes hungry while another gets drunk. Do you not possess houses (*oikias*) for eating and drinking? Do you treat with contempt the church of God (*hē ekklēsia tou theou*) and embarrass those who possess nothing? (11:20-22).

The people addressed here are obviously the more wealthy of the congregation, those who possessed houses of their own. Paul pictures them gathering for what they think is the Lord's Supper, bringing their own food, meats and other dainties. These families of higher status could enjoy table fellowship with other similar families and friends. At the time of the official eating (*en to phagein* of v. 22) of the Lord's Supper, when table fellowship was to include all gathered in the name of Jesus, the rich balked at "rubbing elbows" with the poor. As one scholar points out, "Real table fellowship is somethng quite different from charity at a distance."[2]

Paul's response involves two parallel antitheses. On the one hand Paul contrasts "the Lord's Supper" with each one's "own dinner," on the other, one's "houses" with "the church of God." The basic flaw of these gatherings consisted in the

---

[2]G.Bornkamm, "Lord's Supper and Church in Paul," in *Early Christian Experience*, trans. P.L. Hammer (New York: Harper and Row), p. 128.

failure of some to perceive the meal as the Lord's Supper. By not sharing with the hungry, they were acting as if the event were simply their own dinner. Put another way, they were no longer in their own homes, they were in the church of God—even if in fact they were hosting the church in their homes. In the church of God, the Lord Jesus is the host. The supper is his. Conversely, at the Lord's Supper, the hosting household is no longer simply someone's *oikia*. It is the church of God.

The church of God demands a transformation of the social relationships that separates families during most of the activities of the day. In the church of God everyone has his or her gift to be used for building up the body. No one can despise another, no matter how humble, as unneeded. An organic unity arises, one that can involve extreme diversity.

The answer of Paul in effect relativizes the house church. The attitude that Paul demands might require some spiritual gymnastics. Even the host family, like that of Gaius, might have found it difficult to remember they were no longer in their own household but rather in the church of God. Nevertheless the city-wide assembly afforded some dramatization that one had, at least for a short time, put aside one's own household in order to enter the household of God.

Families from the lowest strata of Corinthian society would not have been able even to have house churches for themselves. They would have had no place for gathering and possibly would not have been able to afford the food for the Lord's Supper, especially if others from non-Christian families were to be present. If the poor wanted to assemble in Christian community in the form of a private house church, they would have had to associate themselves regularly with a particular wealthier family. This could lead to mutually embarrassing situations.

On the other hand, by gathering with the city-wide church, the poor would join in the meal without being dependent on any one family. In the city-wide church the one body could manifest its unity as nourished by the one bread (1 Cor 10:17).

The idea of organic unity dominates the whole treatment

of the assembly in the latter part of 1 Corinthians, but Paul chooses to focus on two social barriers which are broken down in Christ.

> It was in one Spirit that all of us were baptized into one body, whether Jew or Greek, slave or free (1 Cor 12:13).

Paul advocates a gathering in which rich and poor families associate in true table fellowship.

2. Luke-Acts

The stresses evidenced in Paul regarding the house church in the local church help us understand the receding of the household in later New Testament writings. In his portrayal of Paul in Acts, Luke gives us a mixed picture, perhaps because Luke is giving us a mixture of historical traditions and later Lucan theology. Luke still speaks of the households and the hospitality which formed such an important element in the work of Paul (Acts 16:15; 16:33; 18:8; cf. Acts 2:46; 12:12-13). Yet Luke stresses the city-wide church almost to the exclusion of any significance of an individual household.

For Luke the model church was the *koinōnia* of Jerusalem, with its liquidation of private property (Acts 2:42-47; 4:32-35). Here the original twelve form a governing council in the manner of the Jewish Sanhedrin and in turn appoint other city-wide officials (Acts 6:2-6). As the original twelve recede from prominence in Jerusalem, there appears a council of elders (*presbyteroi*) as their collegial successors (15:2.4.6. 22.23).

The Lucan picture of Paul likewise includes his appointment of elders in the churches which he and Barnabas found (14:23). In his last contact with the church of Ephesus, Paul does not meet with the whole church, but rather caucuses with their representative elders, whom he summons like a commander gathering his officers (20:17-18).

The presence of a council of elders, briefly described also

as *episkopoi* (20:28), assures the coherence of the city-wide church, which no longer depends on one household hosting the "whole church," like Gaius of Corinth. The need for all the Christians of a city "to gather in the same place" is no longer urgent, as long as the representative elders could gather in council.

Other details of the Lucan picture of Paul suggest a stress on the city-wide organization. The church of Ephesus (cf. Acts 19) shows many analogies to the city-wide guilds. Paul teaches in the *schola* or lecture hall of Tyrannus (19:9), which sounds very much like the meeting hall of a local guild. Guild halls were often called *scholae* and often named after patrons. Like the leader of a philosophical school, Paul frequently speaks in public places impressing the masses of people by his miraculous power and his rhetoric.

Luke prepares for this deemphasis of the household church by details in his Gospel. Luke drops several of the Marcan references to "house" as a special place in Jesus' ministry (compare Lk 5:17 and Mk 2:1; Lk 11:14 and Mk 3:20; Lk 9:43 and Mk 9:28; Lk 9:46 and Mk 9:33). Luke incorporates Q material which stresses breaking with one's family. Following Jesus takes priority over the most important family obligations, even that of burying one's dead father (Lk 9:59-62; Matt 8:21-22). Christians can expect divisions within the household (Lk 12:51-53; Matt 10:34-36), not just at the end of the world, but "from now on" (Lk 12:52). Whoever loves one's father or mother more than Jesus is simply not a worthy follower (Lk 14:26; Matt 10:37).

3. Ephesians

The other interpreted picture of Paul we have in the New Testament comes from the letters written in the name of Paul after his death. The clearest examples of such "Deutero-Pauline" works are Ephesians and the Pastoral Letters, comprising 1-2 Timothy and Titus. These writings focus on the church. None of these writings show any interest in the private household as the setting for church.

The author of Ephesians copied from Colossians—the surest mark of it not being written by Paul. In this copying, Ephesians duplicates the theme of "universal church," which we examined in Colossians. Unlike Colossians, however, Ephesians makes no reference to a house church or to a city-wide church (cf. Col 4:15-16). Hence the concentration on this heavenly, universal church is greater.

Ephesians is more emphatic about the hierarchical role of the "apostles and prophets." They are the "foundation" on which the church is built (2:20). In this imagery, Christ shifts from being the foundation (cf. 1 Cor 3:11; Col 2:7) to being the capstone. In another interesting shift, Ephesians places the "apostles and prophets" as the mediators of the great revelation of God's mystery. Paul had written to the Colossians:

> The mystery hidden from the ages and from the generations is now revealed to his holy ones ... which is Christ among you (1:26-27).

This idea of the revelation of the mystery to all Christians is found in earlier letters (1 Cor 2:6-12; Rom 16:25-27). Ephesians develops it,

> The mystery of Christ, which was not known in former generations, is now revealed to his holy apostles and prophets in the Spirit, that the Gentiles are co-heirs of the promises of Christ ... (3:4-6).

By inserting a few key words, the author of Ephesians has changed the Pauline theme. Now the object of the revelation is the church, that is, the unity of Jew and Gentile as co-heirs and sharers of the promises. The revelation itself is no longer made to all "his holy ones," but to "his holy apostles and prophets." This group in turn—as evidenced by this letter itself—divulges the secret to all Christians. A conduit of divine grace has been established and it runs through the top officials of the church.

"The apostles and the prophets" appear leading the list of offices in Eph 4:11. They are followed then by "the evangelists and the shepherds and teachers." For the author of Ephesians, the apostles and prophets may be persons of the past. The evangelist would be a contemporary leader working with outsiders. The "shepherd-teacher," an office apparently combining the functions of administration and teaching, remains as the one office within the community. Such a combination of functions would lead to a powerful leader and effective gate-keeper.

Ephesians adds a meditation on the spousal role of the church in regard to Christ (5:22-33). This meditation is in fact an elaboration of the household code Ephesians uses from Colossians (Eph 5:22-6:9; Col 3:18-4:1), incorporating the Old Testament theme of Israel as the spouse of Yahweh (cf. Hosea 3; Ezekiel 16; Canticle). Just as the prophets saw Israel as the (unfaithful) wife of God, so Ephesians sees the church as the faithful and beloved wife of Christ. This imagery reinforces the perspective of the church as the world-wide people of God, the true analogue of Israel.

4. The Pastorals

1 Timothy, 2 Timothy, and Titus appear to be written around the 90s. In these letters the word *ekklēsia* designates the local church, which is "God's household, the church of the living God, the pillar and bulwark of truth" (1 Tim 3:15; cf. 3:5; 5:16). The word no longer means the actual active gathering but rather a stable and solid group of people. No mention is made of this group ever gathering.

Descriptions of the members' activity suggest the life of a philosophical school. Through carefully selected officials, they teach and preach to each other. In addition a common fund helps support needy members (1 Tim 5:16).

These letters reflect a church with serious internal crises, particularly those caused by false teachings. The basic response of the Pastorals is to emphasize positions of authority in the local church. Most important was the "elder-bishop," the chief teacher and manager of the church (1 Tim 3:1-7; Tit 1:5-9). He is the one responsible for maintaining orthodox teaching (1 Tim 5:17; Tit 1:9). The functions which were distributed among various members of the Pauline churches are concentrated even more in the hands of the top offices. A second level administrator is the "deacon" (1 Tim 3:8-12). We are not told what the distinguishing duties of the deacon are. Deacons are consistently spoken of in the plural.

The letter to Titus mentions the appointment "of elders in every town" (1:5), to whom the title "bishop" is given (1:7). According to the Pastorals, then, a local church would have many elder-bishops as well as deacons. A super presiding officer appears in the figures of Timothy and Titus, who are responsible for managing a geographical area, Timothy in Ephesus, Titus on Crete, both of whom are directly appointed to these responsibilities by Paul (1 Tim 1:3; Tit 1:5).

The testing ground for the offices of both elder-bishop and deacon is the private household. Both must distinguish themselves as competent "presiders" (*proistamenoi*) over their own households (1 Tim 3:4.12) before they are chosen to care for "the church of God." Only after proving himself as a good head of his own household can he become *oikonomos* of God (Tit 1:7).

Although a link to the household is thus maintained, in effect a clear distinction is made between the household and the church. The household is the proving ground for work in the church. The role of the elder-bishop or deacon is over and above his role as head of the household.[3]

A link to the household can be seen also in the special responsibility of the elder-bishop to be hospitable (*philoxe-non,* 1 Tim 3:2; Tit 1:8). This crucial function, by which the churches remained in contact with each other, fell on the

---

[3]The analogy of the household and the larger community has its background in Greek thought. Cf. Aristotle, *Politics,* 1252 b 17; Plutarch, *Life of Lycurgus* 19:3. Sophocles writes of the parallel abilities of management. "Whoever shows himself as a useful man in house matters will also prove himself as just in the State." *Antigone* 661-662.

shoulders of this presider and teacher, who apparently was called upon to open his house to visitors from other cities. About fifty years later in Rome, "The Shepherd of Hermas" will speak of an expanded form of the bishop's hospitality, including also the destitute of the community:

> From the tenth mountain . . . are believers such as these: bishops and hospitable men who at all times gladly received the servants of God in their houses without hypocrisy and the bishops who ceaselessly sheltered the destitute and the widows in their ministry.[4]

This connection with the household would indicate a line of development from the patron-administrators of the Pauline church to the elder-bishop of the pastorals. Both would have their office on the basis of their property. Both would need to be heads of households.

On the other hand, in the Pastorals, being head of a household was not the sufficient ground for becoming an elder-bishop. Elder-bishops are to be appointed (*kathistēmi*, Tit 1:5), apparently by a "laying on of hands" (1 Tim 5:22). In this way the connection between the office and the household is loosened.

The connection is further loosened by the community's remuneration of the elder-bishop (1 Tim 5:17).This is not a matter of supporting an itinerant minister in the manner found in the Pauline churches, but a matter of supporting a resident official of the church. The elder-bishop functions less like the propertied patron of the church than a dedicated professional serving and being supported by the community. From the constant admonition for the elder-bishop to avoid greed (1 Tim 3:3; Tit 1:7; cf. 1 Pet 5:2; Acts 20:33-35), we can assume that the position could be lucrative.

The elder-bishops function as a group of presiding officers for the whole congregation of a city. Although involving

[4]*Sim.* IX, 27, 1-2.

their own households in their exercise of hospitality, they functioned each as a *paterfamilias* for the "household of God."

In the Pastorals, private households within the church are a particular area of concern. In some cases the normal household order of financial support is breaking down (1 Tim 5:8.14). More alarming to the author is the way in which households are becoming the seedbeds of heresy. False teachers are "worming their way into homes" seducing "silly women" (2 Tim 3:6). In this way whole households are ruined" (Tit 1:11). Some "women of leisure" are causing trouble "going from house to house ... talking about what they should not" (1 Tim 5:13).

We see here the stereotype of women as irresponsible religious enthusiasts.[5] With the efforts to close the households to bad influences, thus comes an intense anti-feminism. Typified as secondary in creation and primary in sin,

> a woman is to learn in silence and be submissive in all things. I do not permit a woman to teach or to have authority over a man (1 Tim 2:11-12).

The basic thrust of these letters is away from the private household as the place of the church to a city-wide organization, where teaching can be carefully monitored. Authoritative teaching can be assured by authoritative teachers, clearly designated by a line of appointment originating in Paul himself.

This development in the later part of the first century toward strong local authority is best understood against the backdrop of the death of the apostles. While Paul lived, church crises could be resolved by a letter or a visit from the apostle. Churches like those in Corinth could live as a cluster of house churches with little local authority because the powerful authority of Paul could be tapped when needed.

---

[5]Cf. Plato, *Laws*, 909-910; Juvenal, *Satire VI*, 511-592.

Likewise as the apostle above the local church, Paul could maintain the diversity of the gifts and the mutual dependence of all members.

The organization around Paul and his apostolic work resembled in some respects the local *ekklēsia*, with the bond of family-like relationships and the variety of gifts. This apostolic organization, however, differed radically from a local church, running with an almost military tone, centered around one man and his strategies, characterized by a common task rather than a common life, involving co-workers being sent out on mission and reporting back as in a chain of command.

With the death of Paul the apostolic organization with its strong authority structure appears to be absorbed into the local church. Thus the figures of Timothy and Titus, the close co-workers of Paul, loom behind the powerful elder-bishops of the Pastoral letters. The authority of the apostle was no longer above the local church but within it, where it left little room for other gifts and functions. Mutual dependence gave way to hierarchy. Instead of a cluster of families, individually capable of functioning as house church, the local church became the center of church activity.

5. Later Developments

The literary and archeological evidence of the second and third centuries point to the continued development of the church away from the private household toward more elaborately established city-wide churches. Up through the middle of the second century, private residences continued to function as the meeting place for the city-wide communities.

From roughly AD 150 we begin to see adaptations and dedications of private residences for the exclusive use of the church. At this point the buildings should not be considered house churches. These buildings are churches, and soon bear that name.

Archeology does not provide us with much data concerning the last days of the house church, precisely because the house church was not architecturally distinctive. Archeology does show us the rise of the first churches and consistently shows them being adapted from dwellings. The first adaptations consisted of creating larger assembly rooms often with later elaborate provisions being made to separate laity and clergy.[6]

To trace the post-apostolic development away from the house church, we depend very heavily on the literary evidence that comes to us from these times. Perhaps the most important steps to follow the New Testament in that direction are found in the writings of Ignatius of Antioch, who writes around the turn of the second century. In terminology reminiscent of Paul, Ignatius of Antioch addresses the (holy) church which is in Ephesus, Magnesia, or Tralles, or the church of God which is in Philadelphia, Smyrna, or Rome. The universal or "catholic church" is present in each of these places. It is present wherever Jesus Christ is present.[7]

Ignatius speaks of a single bishop who presides over the local church in the name of God.[8] No one should celebrate a

---

[6]White, *Domus Ecclesiae,* pp. 140-240, provides an excellent source of material regarding the archeology of pre-Constantinian churches.

Perhaps the most famous of these excavations is that of "the Christian building" at Dura-Europos. A house built around AD 233 was converted into a dedicated Christian church some seven to twelve years later. The result was a building with an assembly room for some 60 to 70 people and with an elaborate baptistery on the other side of the courtyard. The renovation included no apparent provisions for a congregational meal. Almost for sure no one lived in the building once the renovations were made.

More disputed is the significance of the so-called "house church" of Peter in Capernaum. Archeology uncovered a 5th century octagonal church, some of the walls of which are built on a 4th century Christian sanctuary, which in turn is layered carefully on 2nd century residences. The Franciscan excavator, V.C. Corbo described a part of these residences as "one of the most ancient house churches (perhaps the most ancient) which is known." Cf. Corbo, *House of Peter at Capernaum, a preliminary report,* trans. S. Saller (Jerusalem: Studium Biblicum Franciscanum, 1968), p. 53. The lack of publication of evidence to support this hypothesis leaves other researchers somewhat skeptical.

[7]*Smyrnaeans,* 8,2.

[8]*Magnesians,* 6,1.

eucharistic meal or a baptism without this bishop present.[9] In this church all the important functions are the responsibility of the monarchical bishop, a council of elders, and the deacons.[10] Ignatius leaves no room for a sub-group within the local church.

On the other hand, well into the late second century the memory of the house churches is kept alive in the apocryphal acts. These stories tell of apostles meeting with prominent persons and turning their houses and in particular their dining rooms into places where that apostle would teach and where Christians would regularly assemble.[11] The stories all clearly have as their purpose to establish a line of "apostolic succession" for a local tradition of ecclesiastical authority, but they do so by invoking the memory of the house church— which in the story takes on the traits of a basilica.

The story of Peter in the Pseudo-Clementines describes Theophilus of Antioch, a powerful and wealthy man combining the traits of the local bishop with those of Theophilus of Luke-Acts, who "dedicated the great basilica of his house as a church" where Peter could teach *ex cathedra*.[12] Besides being one of the earliest texts to apply the word "church" to the building, this description is important as a testimony of the fond, even idealized memories of the house church. Yet clearly its purpose is to provide a legend for the founding of the church in Antioch.

An important stage is symbolized by the *Didascalia Apostolorum*, a late third century Christian document. The author instructs bishops:

> Be not harsh nor tyrannical nor wrathful and be not indignant with the people of God delivered into your hands.

[9]*Smyrnaeans,* 8,2.
[10]*Magnesians,* 6,1.
[11]Cf. *Acts of Peter,* 7-8, 19-20; *Acts of Thomas,* 131-133.
[12]*Recognitiones,* X, 71 (PG 1/1453).

We then read an instruction about order and place in the Christian assembly:

> For the elders let there be assigned a place in the eastern part of the house, and let the bishop's chair be set among them, and let the elders sit with him. And again, let the laymen sit in another side of the house toward the east.... When you stand up to pray, the rulers may stand first and after them the laymen and then the women also.... And if any one be found sitting in a place which is not his, let the deacon who is within reprove him and make him to rise up and sit in a place that is proper for him.[13]

In his fourth century *History of the Church,* Eusebius describes the situation of the church in the late third century:

> Who could describe those vast collections of men that flocked to the religion of Christ, and those multitudes crowding in from every city, and the illustrious concourse in the houses of worship? On whose account, not content with the ancient buildings, they erected spacious churches from the foundation in all the cities.[14]

In his *History* Eusebius also reproduces his sermon at the AD 312 consecration of a church in Tyre in which he likens the church building to the holy temple of Israel. He describes the thrones for the presidents and benches for the clergy and a lattice-work chancel to allow the laity to see these leaders. At the center of the building, "noble and grand also and unique is the altar."[15]

These texts not only trace the movement from dining room to noble building, they offer us an insight into the factors behind that development. Numerical growth of membership

---

[13]Ch XII.

[14]*History,* 8,1,5.

[15]*History,* 10,4.

appears as the most obvious reason for the movement to the dedicated church and then to the large building.

Along with this expansion of membership, however, a more significant change involved the Lord's Supper itself. Once the bread and wine ritual was separated from a meal to become "the Eucharist," the community was no longer restricted to a domestic setting. The assembly could move from dining room to assembly hall.

This development of the stylized meal seen as cultic ritual entailed a special shift in the role of the presider. He became the cultic leader who mediated God to the assembly. As the Eucharist was recognized as sacrifice, the leader was seen as priest. A clergy developed—or more precisely a laity developed. Formal patterns of assembly and formal seating arrangements arose.

Eusebius' comparison with the temple points out what is perhaps the underlying dynamism of this whole process. The church sought to reappropriate the cult of the Old Testament. The community sought a temple with an altar. Perhaps we see here an irrepressible quest for holy place.

At a meeting held sometime between AD 360 and 370, a synod of Laodicea forbade the holding of Eucharist in the home:

> Sacrifices should not be offered by bishops or elders in homes (Canon 58).[16]

---

[16]Mansi II, 574C.

Conclusion

The prohibition of Laodicea completes a critical cycle. The Lord's Supper had changed from evening meal to stylized ritual. The assembly had moved from dining room to sacred hall. Leadership had shifted from family members to special clergy. Now the original form of church was declared illegal.

This cycle from house church to basilica epitomizes the dialectic between original vision and later adaptation, between Scripture and Tradition. Jesus in the gospels chose people of various trades for leadership roles. He gathered the crowds on hill sides and lake shores. The later Christians needed a priestly cast of leaders conducting cult in sanctuaries. Paul wrote of the assembly of people as the temple of God; the later Christians understood the temple as a building.

At issue is not a judgment about the value of the development. Such a judgment depends on a personal act of faith in early church traditions, a judgment beyond the scope of this historical study.

What remains an unavoidable judgment in this study, however, is the fact that the basic sense of church did develop. At no point in the development, moreover, did authorities like Paul deem the early communities deficient because of the lack of some later church structure. The historical description of the movement from house church to basilica thus inevitably leads to an understanding of the legitimate possibilities of church as well as to a critique of restrictions on those possibilities. As based on an arbitrary definition of church essence or on an anachronistic picture of Jesus establishing the details of church forms, such restrictions simply do not cut the historical-critical mustard. As based on historical pressures, some restrictions of church form may well have been necessary. As based on historical pressures, however, such restrictions remain open to further developments.

The developments we have seen in the early church follow the fairly typical pattern of the new cults of that day. As a practical necessity these cults and clubs started in private homes, but when able they built their dedicated temples and sanctuaries.

Something in the human heart calls for sacred space. We want to point to a spot as the place of God's presence, just as the Israelites could point to their Holy of Holies as the place of God's glory. We want a place where we can shift religious gears and somehow put behind us the perception of divine absence.

Something in the human heart apparently also longs for sacred people to service these sanctuaries, to assure us that these are truly holy places, and even to represent us in the holy place. The Levitical priests functioned precisely in these ways. Most religions have their professional holy people. Christians quickly developed theirs.

Second century Christianity appears to have longed for the sacred institutions of the Old Testament. The identification of the Christian official as priestly is clearly a reappropriation of a Jewish heritage. The development of the sacred hall with its restricted sanctuary and rigorous rules of ritual is in fact a reappropriation of the Jewish temple.

On the other hand Jesus offended the clergy when he challenged them, "Destroy this temple made of human hands." His message of the Kingdom was in many ways acultic. God's loving presence was to be found in the weeds of the field and in the routine of birds. Love and forgiveness took priority over prayer. The foundation of his "church" was a slow witted fisherman, not a high priest.

Jesus and the Jewish Christians in the decades after Jesus, of course, had their cultic world in Judaism. Perhaps Jesus said little about sacred place and sacred persons because he could presuppose the Jerusalem Temple and an ordained Jewish hierarchy.

Paul, however, told Gentile Christians that they need not become Jews when they broke from their pagan cults. These Christians were to offer their daily lives as living sacrifices. Their very gathering was their Temple.

Earliest Christianity thus involves the dialectic between two concepts of the Temple, one made of people and one made of stones. Such a theological dialectic operates like two divergent lines of force or vectors establishing an actual direction somewhere between the two. The house church of the New Testament may well represent the first vector of this dialectic.

Suggested Readings

Robert Banks. *Paul's Idea of Community. The Early House Churches in their Historical Setting.* Grand Rapids: Eerdmans, 1980.

Raymond E.Brown. *The Churches the Apostles Left Behind.* New York: Paulist, 1984.

_____ *Priest and Bishop. Biblical Reflections.* Paramus: Paulist, 1970.

J.H. Elliott. "Philemon and House Churches," *Bible Today* 22 (1984), 145-150.

F.W. Filson. "The Significance of the Early House Churches," *Journal of Biblical Literature* 58 (1939), 105-112.

E.A. Judge. *The Social Pattern of Christian Groups in the First Century.* London: Tyndale Press, 1960.

Ramsay MacMullen. *Roman Social Relations: 50 BC to AD 284.* New Haven: Yale U. Press, 1974.

Abraham J. Malherbe. *Social Aspects of Early Christianity.* Rockwell Lectures. Baton Rouge: Louisiana State U. Press, 1977.

Wayne A. Meeks. *The First Urban Christians. The Social World of the Apostle Paul.* New Haven: Yale U. Press, 1983.

Jerome Murphy-O'Connor. *St. Paul's Corinth. Texts and Archaeology.* Good News Studies, 6; Wilmington, DE: Glazier, 1983.

J.M. Petersen. "House-Churches in Rome," *Vigiliae Christianae* 23 (1969), 264-272.

Gerd Theissen. *The Social Setting of Pauline Christianity. Essays on Corinth.* Trans. J.H. Schuetz; Philadelphia, Fortress, 1982.

Biblical Index

Old Testament

New Testament